MOM
PhD

 Teresa Bell Kindred is a Christian author, public speaker, and high-school teacher. She is the author of *Mozart for a Mother's Soul, The Knot at the End of Your Rope*, and four Precious Moments gift books. She is a major contributor to *Humor for a Teacher's Heart* and *Cup of Comfort for the Christian Soul*. Kindred is a member of AWSA and enjoys speaking at conferences and retreats. Her column "Kindred Spirits" appears in *Kentucky Living* magazine each month. She and her husband have been married for twenty-four years and have five children.

MOM
PhD

6 Steps to Mastering Leadership Skills for Moms

TERESA BELL KINDRED

HOWARD
PUBLISHING CO.

For Bill
My man of character, with much love

And for Shirley DeMumbrum Bell
My Mom-PhD (1939–1990)

Our purpose at Howard Publishing is to:
- *Increase faith* in the hearts of growing Christians
- *Inspire holiness* in the lives of believers
- *Instill hope* in the hearts of struggling people everywhere

Because He's coming again!

Mom PhD © 2005 by Teresa Bell Kindred
All rights reserved. Printed in the United States of America
Published by Howard Publishing Co., Inc.
3117 North 7th Street, West Monroe, Louisiana 71291-2227
www.howardpublishing.com

05 06 07 08 09 10 11 12 13 14   10 9 8 7 6 5 4 3 2 1

Edited by Ramona Richards and Jennifer Stair
Interior design by Stephanie D. Walker
Cover design by LinDee Loveland

Library of Congress Cataloging-in-Publication Data
Kindred, Teresa B.
     Mom PhD : 6 steps to mastering leadership skills for moms / Teresa Bell Kindred.
        p. cm.
     Includes bibliographical references.
     ISBN: 1-58229-424-0
     1. Motherhood. 2. Motherhood—Religious aspects—Christianity. 3. Parenting. I. Title.

HQ759.K56 2005
248.8'431—dc22
                                                                                2004061683

Some of the names used in the stories in this book are not the actual names; identifying details have been changed to protect anonymity. Any resemblance is purely coincidental.

Scripture quotations not otherwise marked are from the HOLY BIBLE, NEW INTERNATIONAL VERSION®. Copyright © 1973, 1978, 1984 by International Bible Society. Used by permission of Zondervan. All rights reserved. Scriptures marked NLT are from the *Holy Bible, New Living Translation*, copyright © 1996. Used by permission of Tyndale House Publishers, Inc., Wheaton, Illinois 60189. All rights reserved.

Contents

Contents

Foreword

what is a leader?

Just because someone has the title of leader doesn't mean he or she has the skills to lead. Whether it is a mom with her children or the CEO of a Fortune 500 company, the best leadership skills boil down to two basic points: a leader knows where he is going and is able to persuade others to follow.

A mother can lead her children simply because she is their primary caregiver, but if she doesn't have a solid idea of where she is leading them, she will ultimately fail at the most important job in the world—being a godly mom who knows where she is going.

Foreword

My wife, Tee, is the matriarch of Big Oak Ranch and the Croyle household. She has done an awesome job in these two areas, and the fruit of her life is first measured in our biological children, Reagan and Brodie, and the lives of the fifteen hundred children who have called Big Oak Ranch their home over these past twenty-eight years.

We believe leadership skills are more clearly defined as knowing where the correct path is and figuring out the correct way to go down that path. Mastering the skills of being fair, firm, loving, and consistent as we lead our children is the key to being a successful leader.

John Croyle
Author, *Bringing Out the Winner in Your Child*
Founder, Big Oak Ranch

To the
Mom-PhD

Please allow me to introduce myself. My name is Teresa Bell Kindred. My husband, Bill, and I have been married for twenty-four years, and we are blessed with five children ranging in age from twelve to twenty-two. I am a Christian and believe that our Creator formed each of us for a specific reason. I searched for that purpose during my teen years, but it wasn't until after I married and became a mother that I knew without a doubt what God intended for me. I was to tell others about His love and His Son who died for all sinners; and I was to be the best wife and mother I could be.

To the Mom-PhD

Eventually I became a teacher, published writer, and public speaker. I have always been interested in leadership, and when I became a school-board member, I took advantage of the opportunity to attend as many leadership seminars as I could. I'm an avid reader and have studied many recent books about leadership. My personal mission in this book is to encourage mothers and help them improve their leadership skills.

As I worked on this book each day, even before my fingers touched the computer keyboard, I asked God to guide me, to help me find the words to tell you how important you are and how important your mission is. My hope is that this book will encourage you and strengthen your leadership skills, and by doing so, you will become not just a mom but a mom with a plan—a Positive Home Director.

PART *1*

Prep Sessions

Woman, how divine your mission
Here upon our natal sod!
Keep, oh, keep the young heart open
Always to the breath of God!
All true trophies of the ages
Are from mother-love impearled;
For the hand that rocks the cradle
Is that hand that rules the world.

—WILLIAM ROSS WALLACE

Mom—The Positive Home Director

take me to your leader

*Remember your leaders, who spoke the word of
God to you. Consider the outcome of their way of
life and imitate their faith. Jesus Christ is the
same yesterday and today and forever.*

—Hebrews 13:7–8

Remember the old science-fiction movies where a spaceship would land on a strange planet inhabited by little green aliens? Invariably the first words spoken by the crew were "Take me to your leader." Why? Because the leader is the person with authority and the final say-so. The leader is the person who is ultimately responsible for everything that happens in the organization.

If you have a career outside the home, think about your boss. Does he or she have strong leadership skills? If not, that makes your job twice as hard. Working for a leader who doesn't know how to lead is like walking in quicksand. No matter how hard an organization tries to succeed without an effective leader, it will soon become bogged down and sluggish. The organization will never achieve its potential for high standards without strong leadership.

Not only is it important that our leaders have strong leadership skills, but their leadership must be executed in a *positive* way—with lots of encouragement, support, and concrete direction. Negative people sometimes make it to positions of leadership, but the fruit of their leadership is far inferior to that of positive leadership. Those who work or serve under a negative leader may follow out of obligation, but they will likely give only the minimum effort required; their hearts won't really be in their tasks. Positive leaders, on the other hand, know how to inspire those who work with them to higher goals and greater productivity. People who work under a positive leader find personal fulfillment in their work and understand the contribution they make to the bigger picture.

Positive leadership is also needed when raising children. If you are married, you share a leadership position over your children with your husband. If you are a single mom, you are the sole director of your home. Either way, the better leader you are, the better off your children will be.

There is a severe shortage today of positive leaders with strong moral character. Yes, there are some wonderful leaders out there, but we need hundreds, if not thousands more. We need leaders with integrity in politics, schools, churches, the military, and in our communities.

Now ask yourself this vital question about leadership: who is your spiritual leader? As a mom, you lead your children in every aspect of their lives—including their spiritual well-being—and you can't lead them spiritually without a spiritual leader of your own. If you don't have one, please consider making Jesus not only the leader of your life but also your personal Savior. This book is based on principles found in the holy, inspired Bible, and every leadership characteristic we will consider was modeled by Jesus Christ, God's Son.

Be More Than a Mom, Be a Positive Home Director

Hundreds of books have been written about leadership, but few specifically for mothers, the most important leaders of all. In this book, I offer a simple, six-step course in attaining a very special degree—your Positive Home Director degree. At the completion of this course, you will not only be a mom but a Mom-PhD. And our instructor throughout this course will be one of the most esteemed women of all time: the Proverbs 31 Woman. From her we will learn six characteristics that, when applied, will transform you into a Positive Home Director. You will be a mom with a mission, a woman with a plan. Rather than simply *reacting* to the daily situations that arise with your children, you will be a *proactive* leader who has a concrete vision for training and shaping your children to be the men and women God intended them to be.

Most mothers don't think of themselves as leaders. My mother was no exception, yet she was, without a doubt, the most influential person in my life. She instilled in me a love of reading, she taught me that education was the key to the door of opportunity, and, most important, she gave me spiritual roots. She modeled positive leadership skills for my brother and me, yet I'm willing to bet she never thought of herself as a leader.

As moms, we get so bogged down in the day-to-day business of raising a family that we don't feel like leaders of anything, except maybe the cleanup crew. That just isn't the case! If you have children, *you* are their leader. Other than God, you are the most important leader they will ever have.

But in order to *be* important, you have to *feel* important. Many mothers have adopted an "I'm just the mom" mind-set that needs to be replaced with an "I have the most important job in the world" attitude. Modern society and the media are largely responsible for this negative view of motherhood. For example, look at the way we have come to view the word *homemaker*.

In Kentucky, the state where I live, we have "homemakers clubs." Last year I was honored with an invitation to be the keynote speaker at the annual state meeting of the Kentucky

SESSION 1: Mom—The Positive Home Director

Homemakers Association. Before my speech I was conversing with one of the ladies in charge when the topic of membership came up. "Most of our members are older women," she told me. "We have a hard time recruiting young women, and part of the reason is our name: 'homemakers.' It's outdated and old-fashioned. Some states have changed their club's name to something more modern and catchy, but so far we've been unable to convince Kentucky members to do so. I believe that we could reach the younger generation if our club's name wasn't something they associate with their grandmothers."

In other words, being a "homemaker" isn't cool anymore. Or is it? It depends on what standards you use to measure success. While the word itself may be old-fashioned, the definition of what a homemaker does will never be outdated. Yes, we do things differently now than our grandmothers did. Thank goodness we don't have to spend our days hand-washing laundry at the creek or hauling in wood to cook on a wood stove. But while we perform some chores differently, mothers still do many of the same tasks where our children are concerned. Our husbands may help us, or we may hire help, but in most cases, the woman is still in charge of taking care of the home and the children. Mom is the director of her home, as well as the director of finances, the director of information, the director of support services, and the director of nursing. Truly, mothers are VIPs, aren't they?

Being a Positive Home Director may sound complicated and overwhelming, but in this book our respected teacher, the Proverbs 31 Woman, will teach us all the leadership skills we need. Supplementing what we learn from her, we will learn from other women in the Bible, including six "snapshots" of biblical women and the positive leadership skills displayed in their lives.

Hebrews 13:7–8 gives us a clear directive as we begin our six-step course: "Remember your leaders, who spoke the word of God to you. Consider the outcome of their way of life and imitate their faith. Jesus Christ is the same yesterday and today and forever."

That's how we obtain our PhD! We study biblical leaders and the outcome of their lives. Then we imitate their faith and the positive leadership skills they exhibit.

Begin with a Vision

If you were going on a long journey, what would you do before you left home? You would probably research the route you wanted to take and purchase a map or print one from the Internet. Then you would pack a suitcase, empty your refrigerator of perishable items, arrange for someone to care for your plants and pets, and fill your car with gas. You would research the place you were going so you would know what activities you might want to do or places you might want to visit. Then you would embark on your journey. But one thing is sure: you wouldn't leave home until you knew where you wanted to go and had a plan to get there.

Yet every day, babies are born to parents who do not have a family vision. They are raised in homes where parents have not thought about their ultimate goals for their children. Most parents don't know where they are going and don't have a plan to get anywhere.

What is your plan, or vision, for your child? If you don't know or aren't sure, then it's time to decide. Maybe you have a vision, but you just haven't put it into words. If that's the case, then now is the time to get it on paper, think about it, evaluate it, and, if necessary, make additions or changes. If your vision for your children isn't clear to you, you can be sure it won't be clear to them.

Adapt Your Vision to Fit Your Circumstances

Christine Frasier was six months' pregnant when her husband was killed in World War II. Losing a spouse is devastating, but when Christine's circumstances changed, her vision for their son didn't— how she carried out that vision did. She and her husband had spent many hours talking about how they would raise their son to be a Christian, so when Christine's husband was killed, the plan for raising their son changed—but not the vision.

It wasn't easy getting a little boy bathed, dressed, and to church every Sunday by herself, but she did it. During the week she worked forty or more hours at a job that barely met their needs, yet she managed to set a little money aside every month for Jeff's college education. Today Jeff is a minister, and he credits all his accomplishments to the grace of God and the determination and strength of his Christian mother.

Christine had a vision, and she stuck to it even when life threw her a curve ball. Visions remain constant, but strategies for carrying them out may have to change and adapt.

Make God's Vision Your Own

God's vision for His children can be found in John 3:16: "God so loved the world that he gave his one and only Son, that whoever believes in him shall not perish but have eternal life."

The verse first tells us the purpose of God's vision: He loved us, just like we love our children. The second part of the verse states God's vision: to save the world by offering His only Son. Notice that God's vision for His children was followed up by action. His words and actions supported His vision. It won't do us any good to have a vision for our children if we don't follow it up with action.

For example, what good would it do for us to say we want our children to grow up to be strong Christians if we never take them to church or read the Bible with them? Our actions must support our vision, just like God's actions support His.

Write Out Your Family Vision Statement

All companies, boards, and businesses have vision statements so that anyone who comes in contact with their company will know their goals. While a family vision statement would be very different from one written for a company, the process of writing it is the same.

First, consider what a family vision statement is. It is what you hope and pray will happen as a result of your values and convictions. Imagine your child five, ten, or fifteen years from now. That's vision—looking down the road of life and seeing the adult your child will eventually become. Now imagine what characteristics or qualities your child will have. You might want to list those on your vision worksheet, just to get you thinking about what matters most to you.

Keep It Simple

Remember the phrase "Keep it simple"? That's good advice, especially when it comes to vision statements. Before you write your family vision statement, here are a few key points to remember:

- Keep it brief, preferably under ten words. Anything over ten words is too hard to remember.

- Make it catchy and easy to remember. Don't use words that you have to look up in the dictionary. Your vision statement

11

needs to be meaningful for your entire family, and it won't be if your children don't understand it.

- Aim to be inspiring.

- Keep it consistent with your values. Your vision statement should reflect your day-to-day living.

- Clearly describe the adults you want your children to become.

- Make room for flexibility and creativity. Life happens, and from time to time, you will have to adapt. Your vision should allow for those changes.

- Rewrite and edit until you get it just the way you want it.

I am a member of our local school board, yet I can't tell you our school board's vision statement because it's too long. Does your workplace have a vision statement? Do you know what it is? I conducted a very informal poll among friends and family and found out that not one of them could remember their workplace vision statement. Most are simply too long and complicated to be effective.

Learn from the Vision Statements of Others

Take a look at a few vision statements of churches to get a feel for what one looks like. Read them over and then choose the one you think is the most effective.

1. Our church is a lighthouse in our community by spreading the glow of God's love in our world through evangelism, worship, fellowship, discipleship, and ministry.

2. To help people grow to be passionate followers of Christ.

3. Our vision is to see the glory of the Lord fill our city and His kingdom rule established, evidenced by vastly multiplied new believers and healthy churches.

4. With God's blessings and strengthening, we envision our church growing in number and spirit while meeting the needs of the community in such a way as to attract souls to Christ and to encourage their commitment to Him. This commitment leads directly to a ready involvement in and dedication to the church's work and worship.

Which one packed the most powerful punch? Which was the easiest to remember? Most people will choose number two. The other statements say a lot of good things, but if you can't remember the vision statement without having to write it down and carry it around with you, it won't do you any good. Remember, your family vision statement is not the same thing as the actions you will take to make your vision come true. It's not the vehicle you drive on your parenting journey; it's your intended destination.

Give It Some Thought

Take some time to consider the big picture:

- Make sure your statement reflects your ultimate goal for your family.

- Read Proverbs 31:10–31 and try to imagine this woman's family vision statement.

- Make sure you can support your vision statement with action.

- Pray and study the Bible to make sure your vision for your family is in alignment with God's vision for your family.

Let the Bible Inspire Your Vision

1. Train a child in the way he should go, and when he is old he will not turn from it. (Proverbs 22:6)

Training children doesn't mean making their choices for them. It means teaching them how to make their own decisions. If you train your children to make wise choices, they will remain on the right path.

2. Love the LORD your God with all your heart and with all your soul and with all your strength. These commandments that I give you today are to be upon your hearts. Impress them on your children. Talk about them when you sit at home and when you walk along the road, when you lie down and when you get up. Tie them as symbols on your hands and bind them on your foreheads. Write them on the doorframes of your houses and on your gates. (Deuteronomy 6:5–9)

Keep in mind as you write your family vision statement that you are first to love God, then teach your children to follow Him. To do this, your relationship with God has to be part of your everyday life, not just at church. In these verses God is instructing the Hebrews to make sure their children know His commandments, and He wants you to teach your children about Him as well.

3. The rod of correction imparts wisdom, but a child left to himself disgraces his mother. (Proverbs 29:15)

Moms of young children get tired of discipline—so tired that sometimes they give in and give up. When we are tempted to do this, we need to remember that kind, firm correction helps children learn and leads them toward wisdom.

4. Children, obey your parents in the Lord, for this is right. "Honor your father and mother"—which is the first commandment with a promise— "that it may go well with you and that you may enjoy long life on the earth." Fathers, do not exasperate your children; instead, bring them up in the training and instruction of the Lord. (Ephesians 6:1–4)

Parents and children have a responsibility to each other. Children are to honor their parents, and parents should discipline their children with love and patience. Having a strong relationship with Jesus and following Him daily will not only make us better people, it will make parenting easier.

Ready, Set, Write Your Vision

Use the space below to write your family vision statement:

_____

_____

_____

_____

_____

_____

Read the suggestions again for writing a vision statement, and see if your family vision statement is consistent with the guidelines I've shared. Is your statement short, inspiring, and easy to remember? It may take you a few tries to get it exactly the way you want it. When you are satisfied that you have the perfect vision statement for your family, you may want to post it on your refrigerator. When decision-making time comes, reflect on it to make sure your choices will support your vision. Or if you are crafty and can cross-stitch or do calligraphy, why not frame it and put it on the mantel or in your family room?

If your daily life focuses on your vision, then your actions will support it and help you obtain your ultimate goals.

SESSION 1: Mom—The Positive Home Director

Be a Positive Home Director with Vision

Are you ready to begin your pursuit of your PhD degree? In just six, simple sessions, you will have a greater understanding of the woman God wants you to be and how to apply the characteristics of the Virtuous Woman of Proverbs 31 to your own life. But before we begin, be warned that this very capable woman can seem intimidating.

Her purpose is not to make us feel less than perfect. She is given as an example of a very talented woman who cared for her family and her home in such a way that she impressed those around her. And while we may not have all her talents or skills, we can observe her and see how she managed to take care of a home, husband, children, and career in a manner worthy of praise.

Rather than be intimidated by her, we can learn from her. If we have the initiative to improve our leadership skills, this Mom-PhD can be a valuable role model for us.

Reflections on Leadership

1. How important do you think leadership skills are when it comes to parenting? Explain your answer. _____

   _____

   _____

   _____

   _____

   _____

   _____

   _____

   _____

   _____

   _____

   _____

2. List as many leadership skills for moms as you can think of. Choose one that you need to improve upon and tell why. ____

   _____

   _____

   _____

   _____

   _____

   _____

   _____

   _____

   _____

3. Which statement fits your philosophy of motherhood best? "I'm just the mom," or, "I have the most important job in the world." Explain your choice. _____

   _____

   _____

   _____

   _____

   _____

_____

_____

_____

_____

_____

4. How do you feel about the word *homemaker?* Can you think of a word that describes what you do more accurately? _____

_____

_____

_____

_____

_____

_____

_____

5. How does God's vision for us influence your vision for your family?_____

_____

_____

_____

_____

_____

_____

6. Brainstorm some words that you consider key words for family vision statements. _____

_____

_____

_____

_____

_____

_____

7. The statement is made in this chapter, "Moms of young children get tired of discipline—so tired that sometimes they give in and give up." What if anything can be done to alleviate the stress of disciplining your child? What are the dangers of giving in and giving up? _____

_____

_____

_____

_____

_____

_____

_____

_____

_____

_____

_____

8. Why is it important for moms to look ahead and imagine what their children will be five or ten years from now? _____

_____

_____

_____

_____

_____

_____

_____

_____

_____

_____

_____

_____

_____

_____

Encourage one another daily,
as long as it is called Today,
so that none of you may be hardened
by sin's deceitfulness.

— HEBREWS 3:13

The Virtuous Woman

the proverbs 31 woman as a leadership model

*He who finds a wife finds what is good and
receives favor from the LORD.*
—Proverbs 18:22

In this chapter we'll do a quick overview of our upcoming six-step course in leadership skills for moms. We'll look at six traits of the Proverbs 31 Woman—traits that will help us be exemplary wives, mothers, and leaders.

After this overview of our Positive Home Director course, we'll take a closer look at each trait in the following six chapters. As you study these six traits and bring them into your own life, you will become a Positive Home Director, a woman who rises above the rest—a woman with a plan and a vision for her family.

1. She Has Character

A wife of noble character who can find? She is worth far more than rubies. Her husband has full confidence in her and lacks nothing of value. She brings him good, not harm, all the days of her life. (Proverbs 31:10–12)

Our character is what defines us as a person. Can you think of leaders whose character failed to withstand the influence of their position, power, or money? Questionable character destroys a person's effectiveness as a leader—and it can destroy ours too. Leaders who have strong moral character withstand the test of time. The greatest example of this type of leadership is Jesus Christ. No one else has influenced generation after generation the way He has.

The Virtuous Woman is another powerful example of leadership with integrity. Proverbs 31 tells us that the Virtuous Woman is more valuable than rubies. I love the comparison to precious stones, don't you? Even as a little girl, I loved anything shiny and bright. I still have an affection for jewelry, although my tastes have advanced from the rhinestones I played with as a child to jewelry that is a tad more expensive! Comparing the Proverbs 31 Woman to rubies is merely a way to show her worth.

Besides encouraging each other to be women of character, we also need to remind each other of the importance of the task we are doing. No other job (not even president of the United States) has the potential to influence the direction of our families, our communities, and our nation the way motherhood does!

When we become women of character, we also become valuable assets to our husbands. Because of the value our society places on the individual, we have largely ignored the issue of how valuable we are to our spouses and what we can do for them. Remember the old saying "Behind every successful man is a woman"? Isn't that usually the truth? The saying also rings true if you switch the words *man* and *woman*: "Behind every successful woman is a man." Families who support and help each other are much stronger than those where everyone does his or her own thing.

2. She Is Compassionate

She opens her arms to the poor and extends her hands to the needy. (v. 20)

Leaders think of others. If we want our children to know firsthand what it means to be a Good Samaritan, we have to be one.

Every month my friend Leigh Anne visits a nursing home with her three young boys in tow. She doesn't have a relative there. She goes and takes her sons so they will learn to have compassion for the elderly.

If we fail to show compassion for others, how can we expect our children to be compassionate?

3. She Is Competent

When it snows, she has no fear for her household; for all of them are
clothed in scarlet. She makes coverings for her bed; she is clothed
in fine linen and purple. Her husband is respected at the city gate,
where he takes his seat among the elders of the land. She makes linen
garments and sells them, and supplies the merchants with sashes.
She is clothed with strength and dignity; she can laugh
at the days to come. (vv. 21–25)

The Proverbs 31 Woman was prepared. How prepared are you when it comes to parenting? Being ready for whatever happens helps us be more competent. How else could the Virtuous Woman have excelled in so many different areas?

Notice that she is identified as a team player and a helper to her husband. Because of her, he is honored. Do you think she minded sharing the spotlight with her husband? I don't think so. That wasn't the type of woman she was. It probably made her proud that she brought honor to him. Life doesn't always have to be about what we can accomplish for ourselves. It's a great feeling when we can bring honor to those we love.

4. She Is a Communicator

She speaks with wisdom, and faithful instruction
is on her tongue. (v. 26)

Another admirable trait of this working woman was that she was able to deal with the pressures of life with kindness. Notice she didn't yell, cajole, beg, or whine. Our tongues may be a very small part of our bodies, but they can get us into very big trouble. Effective mom-leaders need to control their tongues and improve their communication skills. We need to learn to speak "with wisdom and faithful instruction," like the Virtuous Woman.

Consider, too, that the Proverbs 31 Woman didn't expect others to do her job for her. Leaders delegate, but not when it comes to crucial issues. God gave your children to you, and He wants you to oversee all aspects of their lives. Grandparents and family can be wonderful helpers, but the bottom line is, you are the mom, not Grandma or any other caregiver.

5. She Has Charisma

She selects wool and flax and works with eager hands. . . . She sets about her work vigorously; her arms are strong for her tasks. (vv. 13, 17)

This woman is enthusiastic about the tasks before her! She eagerly enjoys what she does and throws her whole self into life. Charisma just sparkles from her.

Any woman can have charisma if she wants it and is willing to work for it. That doesn't mean we will all be eloquent speakers or have groupies lurking outside our homes waiting for our autographs. But if we follow God's leadership principles and study the examples throughout this book, one day our children will stand and bless us, and our husbands will praise us. It may not happen now. It may not happen during our children's teen years, but it will happen, and when it does, it won't matter that we never made the cover of *Newsweek*. We will have all the reward we need.

6. She Is God Centered

Charm is deceptive, and beauty is fleeting; but a woman who fears the LORD is to be praised. Give her the reward she has earned, and let her works bring her praise at the city gate. (vv. 30–31)

Did you notice that not once in this passage is the Virtuous Woman praised for her physical appearance? Was she a blonde, brunette, or redhead? Was she a size two or a size sixteen? Did she have cellulite or wrinkles? The Bible doesn't say, so we don't have a clue what she looks like, other than what she wore. She was admired, worthy of praise, and precious—and not because she looked like Miss Universe. Women today are bombarded by the message that physical beauty is not only desired, it's a necessary requirement for success, and that just isn't true! Her deeds are what made this woman worthy of praise, not her looks.

Besides, like verse 30 says, physical beauty doesn't last. Boy, oh boy, is that ever the truth. I am forty-eight years old, and that means working twice as hard at looking half as good as I did twenty years ago. The other day I was getting my hair colored, and my hairdresser asked me if I'd ever thought about dyeing my eyebrows.

"What for?" I asked.

"Well," he said, "they are faded. You're hair is a medium brown, and your eyebrows are blond. You can't see them very well."

I couldn't see them at all without my glasses, so I grabbed them from the counter, put them on, and peered in the mirror. He was right! I look at myself every day in the mirror, and I hadn't even noticed I'd lost my eyebrows. "Good grief," I muttered. "If it isn't sagging, it's fading." He laughed and assured me it was just part of maintenance. Hearing the word *maintenance* made me feel like a car that just rolled over 100,000 miles and was in dire need of a tune-up!

We might slow the hands of time by coloring our hair and dyeing our vanishing eyebrows, but we can't stop them. That's why we need to focus on our spiritual self rather than our physical self. Remember, "a woman who fears the LORD is to be praised."

The most important factor in leading children is our spiritual commitment to God and our faith in Jesus Christ. The Virtuous Woman "feared" the Lord. Fear, in this instance, means to respect, trust, and hope.

Jeremiah 17:7–8 says, "Blessed is the man who trusts in the LORD, whose confidence is in him. He will be like a tree planted by the water that sends out its roots by the stream. It does not fear when heat comes; its leaves are always green. It has no worries in a year of drought and never fails to bear fruit."

If we want to bear the fruit of raising caring, confident children, then we must fear God, increase our faith by feeding on His Word, and study the ultimate leader, Jesus Christ. We have to grow our roots deep so that we will be strong and not blown this way and that by winds that try to uproot us from the truth.

Don't Feel Bad: Do Something!

You are the only mother your children have. They can't fire you. They can't renegotiate your contract. They can't hold elections and replace you with someone they like better. Your children look up to you and need you to love and care for them, but they also need you to set the right example and guide them into maturity.

If you feel guilty or inadequate because you think you lack the leadership skills of the Virtuous Woman, don't. These skills are not innate; they are learned. Maybe your mom wasn't a leader, and you've never seen these skills in action. Maybe you're not expected to manage or lead others in your career, so you lack leadership skills you can apply to your family. Maybe you manage people on the job or coach a local soccer team but never realized that you could use these skills to benefit your family. Whatever the reason, guilt won't accomplish anything unless you use it to mobilize yourself into action. Don't feel bad: do something!

Children are impressionable. If we don't give them the leadership they desire and need, someone else will. If you are lucky, the person to whom they turn to fill your shoes might be a wonderful mentor or a loving relative; if you aren't so lucky, it might be an undesirable friend or the neighborhood drug dealer. Your children are too important to leave their leadership to chance. While there are certainly fair shares of kids who grow up under adverse circumstances and rise above their lot, no rational, loving mom wants to make life harder for her children. Our job is to create character and confidence in our children, and we do that by being effective, self-confident, God-fearing Positive Home Directors.

Leadership skills are learned one at a time—trying them on like a new pair of shoes and wearing them awhile until they are broken in and comfortable. You have to learn from your mistakes and applaud your successes. You have to pattern yourself after the Virtuous Woman in Proverbs 31 and other noble women in the Bible. If you are willing to do this, you, too, can be a capable Mom-PhD!

Reflections on the Virtuous Woman

1. Who personally encourages you to be a virtuous woman? How does he or she do this? How can we encourage other women to be virtuous? _____

   _____

   _____

   _____

   _____

   _____

   _____

   _____

   _____

   _____

   _____

   _____

   _____

   _____

2. Look through this chapter and list the different leadership strengths of the Virtuous Woman. Can you think of other strengths that are not listed? Discuss and add the ones you or your group can think of. _____

   _____

   _____

   _____

   _____

   _____

   _____

   _____

   _____

   _____

   _____

3. Colin Powell once said, "There are no secrets to success. It is the result of preparation, hard work, and learning from failure." Do you agree with this statement. Why or why not? How does it apply to motherhood and leadership skills? _____

_____

_____

_____

_____

_____

_____

_____

_____

_____

4. Does the Virtuous Woman intimidate you? Why or why not?

_____

_____

_____

_____

_____

_____

_____

5. After reading about the Virtuous Woman, do you believe the word *homemaker* describes her? Explain your answer. _____

_____

_____

_____

_____

_____

_____

_____

_____

_____

6. "Charm is deceptive, and beauty is fleeting; but a woman who fears the Lord is to be praised." How well do you adjust to the aging process? Do you constantly complain about being overweight, gray hair, and new wrinkles? How can we age gracefully? How much importance should we place on our personal appearance? _____

_____

_____

_____

_____

_____

_____

_____

_____

_____

7. Are you motivated to become a better mother? Can you see how having stronger leadership skills can make you a better mom? Discuss possible ways to strengthen skills and encourage each other as you work your way through the rest of the book. ____

_____

_____

_____

_____

_____

_____

_____

_____

_____

_____

_____

PART 2

6-Step Course

STEP 1
Character:
Leading with Integrity

STEP 2
Compassion:
Leading with Love

STEP 3
Competence:
Leading with Diligence

STEP 4
Communication:
Leading with Wisdom

STEP 5
Charisma:
Leading with Vigor

STEP 6
God-Centered Living:
Leading with Faith

*A good name is more desirable
than great riches; to be esteemed
is better than silver or gold.*

—PROVERBS 22:1

Character

leading with *integrity*

*A wife of noble character who can find? She is worth
far more than rubies. Her husband has full confidence
in her and lacks nothing of value. She brings him
good, not harm, all the days of her life.*
—Proverbs 31:10–12

When I think of a woman with unquestionable character, I think
of my mother. She wasn't perfect, and she would be the first to
admit it, but in her fifty-one years on this earth, she always did her
best to be a woman of character, and I wasn't the only person who
noticed. When she died, the funeral home in our small town filled
with flowers sent by those who wished to convey their sympathy.
In fact, there were so many flower arrangements and potted plants
that we had enough to send to nursing homes and hospitals in sur-
rounding counties. People brought so much food to my home that
we had to freeze most of it, and the day of the funeral there was

standing room only. My mother's death touched people in our community because of the life she lived.

There are many different traits that make up our true character, and we acquire them in numerous ways. We learn from our environment and the type of home in which we grew up. When we are older, we learn by watching others and seeing characteristics we admire in them. If we are lucky, we also come to know that the ultimate source of truth is God and the best place to learn about character building is in the Bible.

Sometimes we may think we know what is right, but God says, "For my thoughts are not your thoughts, neither are your ways my ways" (Isaiah 55:8). We are to live our lives according to His will, not because God is a bossy parent who has to have His way but because He sees things we don't see. He knows things we don't know, and He knows what is best for our lives.

God is always in the same place. Unfortunately, even though He doesn't move, we sometimes do. When we draw away from Him, we lose our ability to see right from wrong. Instead of obedience to His will, we begin to do things our way; and the more we do things "our way," the further away from Him we get. Remember E.T., Steven Spielberg's unforgettable creature from space whose only wish was to "go home"? Well, the good news about God is that we can always go home to Him. He welcomes us with open arms every time, no matter how many mistakes we make.

STEP 1: Character

Our heavenly Father wants us to be women of character, but He leaves the choice up to us. We have to decide for ourselves if we will look to Him for guidance, and then we have to choose whether we will do the right thing.

Do the Right Thing

Do we do the right thing, even when it may not be the popular or safe thing to do?

My mother didn't believe in drinking alcohol, and no matter where she was or whom she was with, no one could change her mind. I once went to New York with her and several of her friends for a short vacation. We dined at some very nice restaurants, and Mom's friends would occasionally have a drink with their meal. No matter how much they teased her or tried to entice her to try just a sip, she resisted. If Mom believed something was wrong, no one could convince her it wasn't. She never changed her principles to suit her surroundings, and neither did another woman of character I have long admired.

She was called Mother Teresa, and in 1994 she gave a speech at the National Prayer Breakfast in Washington, D.C., attended by President and Mrs. Clinton. Her speech said in part, "Any country that accepts abortion is not teaching its people to love, but to use violence to get what they want. This is why the greatest destroyer of love and peace is abortion."[1]

Did Mother Teresa know that President Clinton and the first lady did not share her views on abortion? You bet she did, but it wouldn't have mattered if the room were filled with pro-choice advocates. Her message would have been the same because she knew that God is against abortion, and whatever God is against, she was against. Whatever He is for, she was for. Like Mother Teresa, we have to be women of strong moral character because our children are depending on us.

Pat Tillman is another powerful example of someone who was not afraid to stand up for what he believed in. Pat, a twenty-seven-year-old football player, turned down a multimillion-dollar contract with the Arizona Cardinals to join the U.S. Army because he believed it was the right thing to do. Unlike other men and women today who will do just about anything to be on television, he didn't give interviews about his decision because he didn't want the publicity. Pat thought his decision was no more patriotic than that of other soldiers who volunteered to fight. Not long after he enlisted, Pat was killed in a firefight in Afghanistan. Tillman's life and the choices he made speak volumes about his character.

A biblical example of standing up for what is right occurs in the book of Esther. Born with beauty, brains, and spirituality, Esther was a woman with a lot going for her. In fact, she was so beautiful that King Xerxes took her to be his queen. Esther didn't let her position of authority go to her head nor did she forget her Jewish roots. When a devious plot, devised by a man named Haman, threatened her people, Esther risked her life to save them. She made the king aware of Haman's plot to destroy the Jews, and Haman was hanged on the very gallows he had built for Esther's cousin Mordecai (Esther 7:10).

Esther's decision to tell the king about Haman's plot was more dangerous than it sounds. By law, anyone who approached the king in the inner court without being summoned would be put to death. When Esther told her cousin Mordecai about this law, he reminded her that she was in danger, too, because she was a Jew. He then said, "Who knows but that you have come to royal position for such a time as this?" (Esther 4:14).

When Esther was put to the character test, she passed with flying colors. She didn't ask, "What's in this for me?" She didn't sit back silently while her people faced death, claiming, "It's not my problem." Instead, she asked the Jews to fast for three days while she and her maids did the same. She asked them to pray for God's help in this dangerous endeavor. "When this is done," she continued, "I will go to the king, even though it is against the law. And if I perish, I perish" (Esther 4:16).

Doing the right thing isn't always easy under the best of circumstances, but doing the right thing under adverse circumstances is a true test of character. Esther made an enemy of Haman because of the choice she made. Jesus Christ made enemies because He was determined to follow God's plan. Men and women of character make people without character uncomfortable. If we choose to do the right thing, we shouldn't be surprised if not everyone applauds our decision.

Because we are moms, we need to remember our children are watching every action we take, every decision we make. We have to study the Bible and pray to know what the right thing is, then remain committed to doing it.

Honesty

When an officer of the court swears in a witness, he asks the witness to swear to "tell the truth, the whole truth, and nothing but the truth." If it's important for a witness in a trial to be honest, isn't it even more crucial that leaders be truthful? As the most important leader of all, the Mom-PhD should remember the importance of telling the truth, even when it hurts.

When I was in college, my mother took several of my friends and me to Florida for spring break. When we made the hotel reservations, she insisted on telling them exactly how many people would be staying in each room. My friends complained to me, and I in turn complained to my mother. "But Mom," I argued, "they charge per person. If we tell them that there are only two people in each room, it will be a lot cheaper."

"But that wouldn't be the truth," she said. End of conversation.

Some mothers would have considered telling the hotel that we had two in a room, instead of four or five—a small white lie. Those mothers would be wrong. If my mother had given in and allowed us to lie about how many girls were sharing a room, who knows what effect that might have had on my future decisions? Some thirty years later, I still remember her conviction to always tell the truth, and I strive to do the same.

Another incident that sticks in my mind happened when I was in kindergarten. There were nine girls and one boy in our class. The unfortunate young chap to be in the room with all girls was named Billy, and every one of us had a crush on him. I wanted to impress him so badly that I made up a story about having pet rabbits at my house. Not one or two rabbits, but several, and all in different colors. To this day I don't know why I told such a whopper, but I did. My story worked. Billy was so impressed that he showed up one day with his mother to see my pet rabbits. I remember looking in an old cage we had out in the backyard and saying something like, the bunnies must have gone across the road to visit the neighbor. One lie leads to another lie, and another, and another.

Billy's mother had no idea I was lying and asked my mother about the rabbits. My mother could have played along with me and saved me from an embarrassing ordeal, but, oh no, not my mother! She took me aside, asked me why I had lied, and then marched me straight up to Billy and his mother. I had to admit I had lied, apologize to Billy and his mother, and go to my room for a very, very long time. I still remember the humiliation I felt at being caught in a lie. It definitely wasn't worth it.

We can tell lies with our actions as well as our tongues. Remember Rebekah? She and her husband, Isaac, had twin sons, Jacob and Esau. But Rebekah and Isaac made a costly mistake: they played favorites. "The boys grew up, and Esau became a skillful hunter, a man of the open country, while Jacob was a quiet man, staying among the tents. Isaac, who had a taste for wild game, loved Esau, but Rebekah loved Jacob" (Genesis 25:27–28).

Have you ever known someone who clearly favored one of her children over the others? Favoritism creates animosity and division in a family the way nothing else can. All children have talents and gifts, and each deserves to be loved for who they are, not judged on the basis of what his siblings can or cannot do.

God had told Rebekah, "Two nations are in your womb, and two peoples from within you will be separated; one people will be stronger than the other, and the older will serve the younger" (Genesis 25:23). Esau was born first, then Jacob. Rebekah should have been confident that things would work out; but instead of trusting God, she decided to take matters into her own hands.

Rebekah just couldn't leave things alone. When her husband was on his deathbed, she sinned by encouraging Jacob to pretend to be his brother so that he could receive Esau's blessing. Isaac's eyesight was so bad that Rebekah knew he could only identify Esau by feeling his arms, because Esau was a hairy man and Jacob had smooth skin. She sent Jacob to get two young goats, and she covered Jacob's hands and the smooth part of his neck with the goatskins so he would be hairy, like Esau. Her plan worked, and Isaac was deceived by Jacob's disguise. Jacob tricked Isaac into giving him Esau's blessing, but Rebekah and Jacob paid a hefty price for their sin.

Esau was furious and threatened to kill his brother, so Rebekah had to send Jacob away. She never again saw the son she loved so much. What a mess her favoritism, trickery, lies, and jealousy had created!

Instill a Love for Truth

Nothing can do more damage to a mother's character than saying one thing and doing another. People of character simply do not do this. If you give your children one set of standards to live by while you live by another, your children know it. Your actions will influence their decisions more than your words.

How much influence would the coach of a basketball team have over his players if he got drunk every night, smoked pot, and came in late to practice every day? Let's say that then, once he got to practice, he admonished the players to stay in shape, be on time, and stay away from anything illegal. Would they do it? Would they respect him? No way.

Now let's suppose there is another basketball team whose coach is in excellent physical condition. He's at practice every day on time and is known as a family man, one who never drinks, smokes, or does anything even remotely questionable. When this coach talks to his team about the importance of character, honesty, and integrity, do you think they will listen? You bet.

On the other hand, does having a great coach with impeccable character mean that every player will model himself after the coach? Nope. There are no guarantees in ball teams or in parenting. No matter how good a mother you are, even if you have exceptionally high standards and are a very virtuous woman, your children will still make mistakes. But children's mistakes are less likely to be serious if their mother is a godly woman with high moral standards than if she is not.

Scripture tells of a woman named Herodias, whose character led her to make choices that had serious consequences. King Herod had divorced his wife to marry Herodias, who was his half brother Philip's wife. John the Baptist was a popular preacher at the time whose ministry had thousands of followers. When he pointed out that it was unlawful for Herod to marry Herodias, she was furious. (This is a perfect example of a person with character making a person without character very uncomfortable!) When Herod held a birthday party and invited all his friends, Herodias's daughter happened to be the entertainment for the night. After she danced for them, Herod was so pleased with her performance that he boasted in front of his friends and said, "Ask me for anything you want, and I'll give it to you."

The girl ran to her mother and wanted advice. "What shall I ask for?"

"The head of John the Baptist," Herodias answered.

At once the girl hurried back to the king with the request: "I want you to give me right now the head of John the Baptist on a platter."

So because the king had boasted in front of his friends and wasn't willing to back down on his word, John the Baptist was beheaded (see Matthew 14).

Talk about poor judgment and lack of character! Herodias was mad and wanted revenge, so she used her daughter to get it. We have to be women of character for our children's sake because just as Herodias's daughter looked to her for advice, our children are looking to us to lead them.

I read a story once about a young mother who was trying to clean her house while her four-year-old followed along behind her. Every time she took a step, he took a step. Finally, when she had tripped over him for the third time, she stopped and asked with exasperation in her voice, "What are you doing? You are right under my feet!"

He looked up at her with big, round eyes and said softly, "My Sunday school teacher said I should follow in Jesus's footsteps, but since I can't see Him, I'm trying to walk in yours."

Our children are trying to walk in our footsteps. If we are women of character, we will walk in Jesus's footsteps so that we can have a positive influence on others.

A Servant's Heart

In a day and time when so many are me-centered, Positive Home Directors are to be humble servants. Just like the word *homemaker* isn't popular anymore, the idea of being a servant is no longer popular either. We want others to serve us. We have become accustomed to being waited on, and we like it.

A leader who expects the world to revolve around her wants and desires won't be respected for long. We have to realize that humility is an extremely important quality of positive leadership. Remember when Jesus washed His disciples' feet before the Last Supper? When He was done He said, "I have set you an example that you should do as I have done for you" (John 13:15). Jesus wants us to humbly serve one another.

Think about the Virtuous Woman. Was she proud or boastful? No. She went about humbly serving her family and her community, and they loved her for it.

In Acts we are told about another woman who had a servant's heart. Her name was Dorcas. She "was always doing good and helping the poor" (Acts 9:36). Everyone who knew Dorcas loved her, and when she died, her friends asked Peter to come at once. Peter was taken to the room where her body lay. "All the widows stood around him, crying and showing him the robes and other clothing that Dorcas had made while she was still with them" (v. 39).

Peter prayed and raised her from the dead. Then he called the believers and the widows and presented Dorcas to them alive. This became known all over Joppa, and many people believed in the Lord (vv. 41–42). Because Dorcas served others and because Peter raised her from the dead, she led others to the most perfect servant of all, Jesus Christ. We can do the same thing.

SNAPSHOT OF A WOMAN OF CHARACTER
A Mother Willing to Sacrifice

Two prostitutes came before King Solomon with a problem. Both of them had given birth about the same time and were staying in a house together. One mother had accidentally killed her baby during the night because she "lay on him," probably suffocating him. She then took the dead baby and switched it with the other woman's baby while that mother slept. Now they stood before Solomon with one live baby and a very big problem: both of them claimed the baby was theirs. One of them was lying. It was up to Solomon to decide which one (see 1 Kings 3).

Solomon solved the problem by asking for his sword and offering to divide the baby. One woman agreed, but the other pleaded, "Please, my lord, give her the living baby! Don't kill him!" (1 Kings 3:26).

Solomon immediately knew which woman was the mother of the living baby because it was obvious which woman loved the baby. The mother who was willing to give up her child exhibited a strength of character that manifested itself in her willingness to make sacrifices.

Kara, a friend who for years has been trying to have a child of her own, recently was present at her daughter's birth. What's unusual about that, you ask? Kara didn't give birth to her daughter; someone else did. Instead of choosing abortion, this young girl loved her baby enough to place her in a good Christian home. I'm sure it wasn't easy for the girl to give birth and then place her newborn daughter in Kara's arms, but she didn't carry a child for nine months and give her up because it was the easy solution to her problem. She did it because it was the best thing for the child.

Reflections on Character

1. How important do you personally think character is when it comes to leadership? Defend your position. _____

_____

_____

_____

_____

_____

_____

_____

_____

_____

2. Think of someone you know who always tries to do the right thing. How is this person viewed by others in his or her home, church, community? _____

_____

_____

_____

_____

_____

_____

_____

_____

3. Is there a difference in what we think is the right thing and what God thinks is the right thing? _____

_____

_____

_____

_____

_____

4. Look up at least five verses that show how God feels about the importance of telling the truth. _____

_____

_____

_____

_____

_____

_____

_____

_____

_____

_____

_____

_____

5. Rebekah was a mother who played favorites. What are some possible dangers of having a favorite child?_____

_____

_____

_____

_____

_____

_____

_____

_____

6. Name some ways mothers can teach their children to love the truth._____

_____

_____

_____

_____

_____

_____

_____

7. How can we teach our children to be servants in a "me-centered" world? _____

_____

_____

_____

_____

_____

_____

_____

_____

_____

8. The best choice for our children is not always the easiest choice. Think of a difficult decision you have made concerning your child. What motivated you to choose the hard way instead of the easy way? _____

_____

_____

_____

_____

_____

_____

_____

_____

_____

_____

_____

_____

_____

Therefore, as God's chosen people, holy and dearly loved, clothe yourselves with compassion, kindness, humility, gentleness and patience. Bear with each other and forgive whatever grievances you may have against one another. Forgive as the Lord forgave you. And over all these virtues put on love, which binds them all together in perfect unity.

—COLOSSIANS 3:12–14

Compassion
leading with *love*

She opens her arms to the poor and
extends her hands to the needy.
—Proverbs 31:20

I thought I knew everything there was to know about love—
then I became a mother. The love of a mother for her child is
very different from any other kind of love. For example, I love
my husband, but I have never held his foot in my hand (like I
did my babies) and kissed each little toe (for obvious reasons!).
If I lie awake at night and stare at my husband, it's because he's
snoring so loudly I can't sleep. Yet many, many nights I have
crept into my children's bedrooms to see their angelic faces
peaceful with slumber, especially when they were babies. No
matter how long I stared at them, I just couldn't believe the

miracles God had allowed Bill and me to take part in. I confess that just a week or so ago my daughter was home from college, and I sneaked into her room, knelt beside her bed, and watched her sleep.

I don't pretend to know how motherhood affects all women, but I know without a doubt that motherhood changed me. Because I wanted my children to be committed to Christ, I became a stronger Christian. Being a mom has taught me the power of prayer and reminded me that even though I am weak, He is strong. In fact, God's love for us is so strong that He sent His only Son to die on the cross for our sins. He showed us what the power of love can do. All moms can plug into that power source.

Jesus said, " 'Love the Lord your God with all your heart and with all your soul and with all your mind.' This is the first and greatest commandment. And the second is like it; 'Love your neighbor as yourself'" (Matthew 22:37–39).

John 3:16 says, "For God *so loved* the world that he gave his one and only Son, that whoever believes in him shall not perish but have eternal life" (emphasis added). Because God loved us, He sent His Son to save us. What does He expect in return? For us to keep His commandments—and He commands that we love!

The Virtuous Woman knew how to lead with love. Besides taking care of her family, she "extends her hands to the needy"

(Proverbs 31:20). She was a compassionate person and a great example of what "love leadership" can do.

Love Leadership

When Paul wrote to the Christians at Corinth, he gave them some very important advice that we can use as a model on how to love:

If I speak in the tongues of men and of angels, but have not love,
I am only a resounding gong or a clanging cymbal. If I have the
gift of prophecy and can fathom all mysteries and all knowledge,
and if I have a faith that can move mountains, but have not love,
I am nothing. If I give all I possess to the poor and surrender
my body to the flames, but have not love, I gain nothing.

(1 Corinthians 13:1–3)

Have you ever thought about what it would feel like if no one had ever loved you? Think about it for a moment. Most of us have families where we experience love on a daily basis. We grew up in homes where at least one person loved us. We have church families where we love our brothers and sisters in Christ. But what if you had never experienced love? What if no one had ever taken care of you when you were sick, fed you when you were hungry, or visited with you when you were lonely? How would you know what love is?

I can't answer that question from my own experience, but I have seen what living without love can do through students who have passed through my classroom over the years. Some of them had known love for a short time, only to have it taken away. Others had never experienced love at all.

Dave Pelzer wrote several books about living without love. In his book *A Child Called "IT,"* you can read about his emptiness. Through his words you can learn about the pain of being treated as nothing. His abusive mother starved him, burned him, and more. Dave's second book, *The Lost Boy*, continues his life story by detailing his search for love and his experiences as a foster child. *A Man Named Dave* is the story of his recovery and how he overcame his childhood. Dave fought his way through those terrible years, and like a flower that grows out of a crack in the sidewalk, he grew until he found love.

Love is the most essential ingredient to motherhood, and it should be the basis for everything moms do. Most mothers love their children, but not all mothers act on that love the way God intends for them to. Maybe that's because they don't know or don't understand how to lead with love. If that's the case, then this chapter describes in detail the characteristics that define what love is all about.

Love Leadership Is Patient and Kind

Love is patient, love is kind. (v. 4)

Do we strive to be patient and kind mothers, or do we try to motivate our children by yelling or shouting? Can a child feel love when they are being screamed at? What do they learn from a mother who constantly loses her patience? Even the tone of a mother's voice carries a message.

My friend Elise has the softest, gentlest voice imaginable. I have never heard her talk to her daughters in any other tone. Her girls are two of the most respectful young ladies I've ever met, and they talk in the same soft manner as their mother.

Another lady I know, Janine, doesn't exactly yell at her children, but she speaks very loudly and consistently threatens them with what will happen to them if they don't do as she wishes. Her children are loud and demanding. Rarely do they obey Janine the first time she asks them to do something. She threatens; then they argue. This pattern is repeated over and over.

Both Elise and Janine love their children. Both are concerned and caring parents. Janine may not even realize how her voice sounds to others or how loudly she speaks, but her actions are reflected in her children's behavior.

The next time you talk to your children, try to hear yourself the way others hear you. It not only matters what we say, but also how we say it.

Love Leadership Does Not Boast

[Love] does not envy, it does not boast, it is not proud. (v. 4)

Have you seen any political ads lately? No boasting or bragging there, right? I suppose we could assume the candidates are merely stating the facts as they see them. Still, I think it might greatly improve political advertisements if every candidate had to apply to their campaign the attributes of love found in 1 Corinthians 13.

What about moms? Can we learn anything from these verses? You bet we can.

Children learn what they live. If we don't want our children to be envious, then we can't envy others. If we don't want them to boast or brag, then neither should we. That doesn't mean we can't be proud of their achievements. It simply means we should have a humble heart and teach our children that humility is a virtue. And that isn't an easy thing to do in today's me-centered world. If we aren't careful, our children will think humility is for losers because many popular role models today aren't exactly humble. That's why it's so critical that as moms we first tell our children what humility is and then show them how it looks.

Often young children go through a stage where they have to outdo their friends. One child will say something like, "My daddy has a big truck." The other child will answer back, "Oh, yeah? Well, my daddy has a bigger truck than your daddy." And so on and so forth.

Sometimes we adults play the same game, even though we should know better. Everything we own will one day rust, rot, or fall to pieces. Not a pleasant thought, but true. We don't really own anything; we just accumulate things for a while and then leave them behind when we die.

Humility is desirable, while being envious and boasting isn't. How do I know? Because James tells us, "Humble yourselves before the Lord, and he will lift you up" (James 4:10). Now that's the kind of spiritual power boost I want! How about you?

Love Leadership Is Not Rude

[Love] is not rude, it is not self-seeking, it is not easily angered. (v. 5)

Are we ever rude to our children? It happens occasionally if we are tired or stressed, but if it happens consistently, there is a problem. Our children will learn how to be rude by watching us be rude to others.

Have you ever had a car pull out in front of you, and before you knew it, you were honking your horn and yelling? Or what if someone is rude to your child? Are you automatically rude back? At times we may genuinely need to defend our children, but we must be careful how we defend them.

How did Jesus respond to those who were rude to Him? He wasn't rude or angry in return. His actions were not self-seeking; they were selfless. Jesus didn't go to the cross because He wanted to. He went because His Father wanted Him to. He went for you and me and our sins. Real love—the kind of love talked about in 1 Corinthians 13—thinks of others first, self last.

Love Leadership Forgives and Forgets

[Love] keeps no record of wrongs. (v. 5)

God doesn't want us to be a keeper of past wrongs. A lady I know, we'll call her Beth, has five children, ten grown grandchildren, and two great-grandchildren. She and her husband have been divorced for years, and Beth lives alone. Even though her family lives close, she rarely sees any of them. Over the years her vicious temper and her inability to forgive and forget have alienated her from everyone who ever loved her. I am a friend of one of Beth's daughters, Ellen. Her relationship with her mother breaks my heart.

"Every time one of us kids or Dad did something she didn't like, Mom would go berserk and say horrible, hurtful things," remembers Ellen. "Then she would bring stuff up from years ago, stupid things that everyone else has forgotten. I don't know how anyone can stay mad for forty or fifty years, but she has. We just got tired of fighting with her all the time, so we stopped trying to have family get-togethers. It wasn't worth it."

Because of her anger and inability to forgive and forget, Beth lost her family. What a horrible price to pay.

Love Leadership Rejoices with the Truth

Love does not delight in evil but rejoices with the truth. (v. 6)

Little children are often painfully truthful. If you don't believe me, just ask my sister-in-law, Kelly. She was managing a small grocery store, and her then six-year-old son, Thomas, was often close by her side. One day Thomas went up to an employee and peered behind him. The employee looked around to see what Thomas was looking at. When he didn't see anything, he asked Thomas just what he was staring at.

"Mama said you moved so slow she was going to light a fire under you. I was just looking for the fire," he replied.

I'm not sure Kelly rejoiced that Thomas had told the truth that day!

Teaching our children to love what is good and to be honest is essential, especially when we live in a society that doesn't always value goodness and truth. If we lead with love, we do not take pleasure in evil or in others' mistakes, but we rejoice in the truth and in those who do God's will.

Love Leadership Always Perseveres

[Love] always protects, always trusts, always hopes and always perseveres. (v. 7)

This verse outlines four powerful "always" characteristics of love leadership. Let's look at each characteristic in closer detail.

Love Always Protects

When our son Justin was about seven years old, he was playing outside one summer day and a bumblebee flew under his T-shirt. He ran toward the house crying and screaming, and his aunt Kelly happened to pull up in the driveway about that same time. Quickly realizing what the problem was, she grabbed Justin, stuck her hand under his T-shirt, and caught the bee, saving him from any more stings. Kelly didn't stop to worry about whether she would get stung herself. She acted on Mom-PhD instinct.

We can't protect our children from everything—but we do have the power of prayer on our side, and God listens. That doesn't mean that nothing bad will ever happen to our children if we pray for God to protect them. But Matthew 18:10 does teach that all children have angels who are watching them: "For I tell you that their angels in heaven always see the face of my Father in heaven." And one day, those who neglect and abuse children will pay for their actions. Until then, we Positive Home Directors have a responsibility not only to protect our own children as best we can but to watch out for the needs of other children as well.

Teachers and those in the education field are required by law to report neglect or abuse of children. God's law requires that we do the same. Looking the other way or making the excuse that we don't want to get involved is not what love is about. Love leadership "always protects."

Love Always Trusts

The familiar hymn "Trust and Obey" says, "There's no other way, to be happy in Jesus, but to trust and obey." The hymn is right.

Love and trust should be synonymous. Have you ever known a husband and wife who don't trust each other? Without trust a marriage is doomed. Trust is a building block of love.

If we love our children, then we should trust them. I was reminded of this not long ago. We live in a very small community where everyone knows everyone else's business. Sometimes being a close-knit community is great, and sometimes it feels like living in a fishbowl. If my children make a mistake, they can be assured that sooner or later (and usually sooner) I'm going to hear about it. I was surprised when a close friend told me that my child had lied to me, but because she was a close friend and she seemed so sure of her information, I believed her.

Instead of questioning my child calmly, I accused him of lying. After a few seconds of silence and a look of surprise that I knew was sincere, he told me I was mistaken and informed me of what had really happened. My child hadn't lied to me. I had placed my trust in the wrong person, and as a result, I felt terrible, and so did my falsely accused child. Trust is a fragile thing, and I made a mistake in the way I handled the situation. Next time I will presume my child is innocent until proven guilty, the way I should have the first time.

Love Always Hopes

When things are bad, hope is the single thread we hold on to. Hope is the reason there were survivors of Nazi concentration camps. Our nation was founded on the hope that we would have the freedoms and privileges our founding fathers had been denied. Hope in the Lord is a way to renew our strength when we are weary.

"But those who hope in the LORD will renew their strength. They will soar on wings like eagles; they will run and not grow weary, they will walk and not be faint" (Isaiah 40:31). Moms get tired, but God never does. That's why we can trust Him to lead us. If His strength is the source of our strength, then we can call upon Him for help. When we hope in the Lord, we know that His promise of strength will carry us through, whether we are tired, distressed, or discouraged.

Love Always Perseveres

Perseverance has been defined as "the patient endurance of hardship; persisting in a state or enterprise in spite of difficulties and discouragement."[1] Doesn't sound too pleasant, does it? James 1:2–3 says, "Consider it pure joy, my brothers, whenever you face trials of many kinds, because you know that the testing of your faith develops perseverance."

When all five of my children were young, I thought that if I persevered through the diapers, bottles, and potty-training years, my life would be easier. Boy, was I ever wrong. Those years were nothing compared to life with five teenagers. As moms, one of our toughest challenges is to persevere throughout our children's teen years. Their hormones are exploding just at the time when ours have decided to give us hot flashes and a roller-coaster ride of emotions.

The other day I took three of my own teens and two of their friends to the mall. (Be warned: During the teen years, kids travel in packs. They don't do anything alone. No matter where we go, they insist on taking friends with them!) So on this particular day, I was navigating the busy interstate with five teenagers in my car. They insisted that we listen to something on the radio. (They called it music, but it wasn't.) They turned up the bass until it vibrated throughout my whole body. I turned it down; they turned it up. I switched the station; they switched it back. Finally I decided it was more important to concentrate on my driving than to fight over the radio, so I gripped the steering wheel until my knuckles turned white and forged ahead. The six of us trooped into the mall, and since I had the credit cards, they stuck with me. Would you believe that every store we went in played the same loud, abrasive stuff that I was forced to listen to in my car? By the time we left the mall, every hair on my head was standing on end, and I just knew I was going to jump out of my skin any second.

Karen O'Connor is a friend of mine, and she wrote a book

called *Gettin' Old Ain't for Wimps*. Well, Karen, raising teenagers isn't for wimps either, but with God's help (and earplugs!), we will persevere.

Love Leadership Never Gives Up

Love never fails. (v. 8)

Imagine you are in a race with other moms. The race begins and you take off running, determined to get to the finish line first. After a while you get tired. As you round the corner and enter the home stretch, you lose momentum and fall behind. Pretty soon it becomes evident that there is no way you are going to win. Do you give up and sit on the sidelines, or do you hang in there, determined that you will finish the course laid before you?

According to Hebrews 12:1–3, we should *"run with perseverance* (there's that word again!) the race marked out for us. Let us fix our eyes on Jesus, the author and perfecter of our faith, who for the joy set before him endured the cross, scorning its shame, and sat down at the right hand of the throne of God. Consider him who endured such opposition from sinful men, so that you will not grow weary and lose heart"* (emphasis added).

When it comes to raising children, we are in the most important race of our life. No matter how tired, discouraged, or down we get, we can't give up because giving up is failure. We have to stay in the race and fix our eyes on Jesus, the author and perfecter of our faith.

Love never fails because it never gives up.

The kind of love Paul is speaking of is impossible to practice without God's help. It is a love that gives while expecting nothing in return. The more Christlike we are, the closer we are to understanding what love leadership is. Christ consistently reached out to others. He was unselfish and focused not on His needs, but on the needs of others—the same way a mother unselfishly devotes herself to her children and puts their needs before hers.

Love Leadership Demonstrates Love

And now these three remain: faith, hope and love.
But the greatest of these is love. (v. 13)

Faith in God is the foundation of love leadership. Hope is the attitude we should have. Love is the verb. It is the action behind faith and hope.

To say "I love you" is one thing. To show someone your love is another. I wrote the following poem for my mother, and I believe it illustrates well the actions of a Christian mother.

> *When you are young, she is cookies and milk after school.*
> *She is a comforting hug after a bad dream in the middle of*
> *   the night.*
> *She is the cold rag on a feverish forehead.*
> *A calm strength when you are frightened.*

By the time you are a teenager, she is nosy and bossy.

She has more advice than Dear Abby.

She is old and out of touch.

She insists you go to church and prays daily you will not stray too far from the principles she has taught you.

She is the first to jump to your defense when someone criticizes you, and the first to tell you when you are wrong.

Years pass. You are a young woman, and it is your wedding day.

She is more than your mother; she is your friend, and she rejoices at your happiness.

The proud look on her face tells the world how much she loves you.

When she becomes a grandmother, the advice she gave you when you were a child suddenly takes on new meaning.

She never tires of hearing about her grandchildren's antics or accomplishments, and she relishes in relating stories about them over and over to anyone who will listen.

When she holds her grandchild in her arms, you see the same look of love on her face that was there for you when you were a child.

More years pass and time begins to take its toll.

Her hair is now gray and her face lined with wrinkles. Her eyesight and hearing are failing.

Her body is bent and her step unsure.

She is forgetful and frail and then one day . . . she is gone.

She is memories of comforting hugs in the middle of the night, cookies and milk after school, the proud look on her face the day of your wedding, the loving way she held your child.

She is gone, and yet she is with you because when you look in the mirror, you see the woman she molded, and the

*little girl who still longs to run to the comfort of her
    mother's arms.*
*Now it is your turn to do the things she did, and when you
    do them*
*You remember her love and realize that at last you know
    her secret.*
A mother is mortal, with imperfections and failings.
*She cannot solve the problems of the universe, nor can she
    protect her children from every danger. She can only try.*
*You wish with all your heart that you could tell her thank
    you one more time.*
*And you can almost hear her whisper, "Thank me by lov-
    ing your children as much as I loved you."*
She has given you something priceless,
The legacy of her love.

How do we show our children we love them? Mothers don't just say the words "I love you"; they demonstrate their love to their children every day. God didn't just say He loved us; He sent His only Son to die for our sins. Christ didn't just say He loved us; He suffered and died on the cross so that we could have a home with Him in heaven someday.

Love leadership is the greatest leadership style ever known to man, and Christ brought it to us from His Father. You can read about the gift of love in 1 John 4:7–8: "Dear friends, let us love one another, for love comes from God. Everyone who loves has been born of God and knows God. Whoever does not love does not know God, because God is love." Children need to know this special kind of love, and they need to learn about it from their family. Do our children see us loving others the way God wants us to? Are you a compassionate person?

Verses 20–21 of this same chapter say, "If anyone says, 'I love God,' yet hates his brother, he is a liar. For anyone who does not love his brother, whom he has seen, cannot love God, whom he has not seen. And he has given us this command: Whoever loves God must also love his brother."

If we genuinely love others the way God wants us to, our children will know it because they'll see it. And if we have that kind of love, then we can be sure we are leading our children down the same path the Virtuous Woman led hers.

SNAPSHOT OF A COMPASSIONATE WOMAN
Jochebed

It's hard to imagine the difficult circumstances Jochebed found herself in. Because she was a Hebrew living in Egypt when she gave birth to a son, she knew he would be killed. Pharaoh had ordered that all newborn baby boys should be thrown into the Nile. Girls were allowed to live, but not boys.

Jochebed's love and compassion for her son moved her to place her infant in a tiny papyrus basket on the river. Her compassion was stronger than her fear of the king. Rather than doing nothing and accepting the king's evil decree, she had compassion on her child and took action. Have you ever heard someone make the following statement (usually accompanied by a heavy sigh): "I wish such-and-such were different (sigh), but there's nothing I can do."

Baloney! Hogwash! Fiddlesticks!

There's always something you can do. If God is on your side, "all things are possible" (Matthew 19:26).

Jochebed took a chance. She could have been killed for hiding her son. He could have been killed; and if he had been, at least she would have had the satisfaction of knowing she tried.

Being paralyzed with fear does no one any good, especially in the face of something or someone as evil as this pharaoh.

The baby whom Jochebed placed in the basket was Moses, and when Pharaoh's daughter found the baby, she, too, took compassion on him and adopted him as her own and chose Jochebed to nurse the baby. Because Jochebed's compassion moved her to do something instead of nothing, her baby was saved. God places opportunities for compassion in front of us every day. Whether we recognize them or ignore them is up to us.

Reflections on Compassion

1. Who do you consider a very compassionate person? What characteristics do they exhibit that illustrate their compassion? ___

   _____

   _____

   _____

   _____

   _____

   _____

   _____

   _____

2. Name some possible results of not having a loving mother (or mother figure) in a home. _____

   _____

   _____

   _____

   _____

   _____

   _____

   _____

   _____

3. How can our tone of voice and mannerisms convey love?

   _____

   _____

   _____

   _____

   _____

   _____

   _____

   _____

4. Is it possible to be a leader and be humble? If so, how? Should we teach our children humility? If so, how?_____

_____

_____

_____

_____

_____

_____

_____

_____

5. Research some verses from the Bible that discuss humility.

_____

_____

_____

_____

_____

_____

_____

_____

6. How easy is it for you to forgive and forget? What does the Bible teach about forgiveness? What are some possible consequences of not forgiving others? _____

_____

_____

_____

_____

_____

_____

_____

_____

_____

7. Do you agree with the following statement? "Looking the other way or making the excuse that we don't want to get involved is

not what love is about." Why or why not? _____

_____

_____

_____

_____

_____

_____

8. Name a difficult situation that "hope" helped get you through.

_____

_____

_____

_____

_____

_____

9. What does the word *persevere* mean to you as a mother? As a leader? As a Christian?_____

_____

_____

_____

_____

_____

_____

10. Read the poem near the end of step 2 that I wrote about my mother. Now try writing a short poem of your own about your mother or about the way you feel about being a mother. Share it with your group or your husband and children. _____

_____

_____

_____

_____

_____

_____

_____

A wise woman builds her house,
but with her own hands
the foolish one tears hers down.

—PROVERBS 14:1

Competence
leading with *diligence*

When it snows, she has no fear for her household;
for all of them are clothed in scarlet. She makes
coverings for her bed; . . . She is clothed with strength
and dignity; she can laugh at the days to come.
—Proverbs 31:21–22, 25

When my first child was born, I probably knew less about mothering than most. I still remember the sense of panic I felt when the nurse brought my newborn son into my hospital room and left me to dress him and take him home. I didn't have a clue where to start! As I looked at my son's sweet, innocent face, I realized that though I didn't know a thing about being a mother, my son didn't know that. I was the only mom he had, and he was counting on me. For some reason that made me feel better, and I calmed down.

None of us is born knowing everything about child rearing. What we do know we learn from our environment, role models, and society. Some of us were raised in nurturing environments with loving mothers who modeled successful parenting skills, and others of us were not so fortunate. While all moms have different backgrounds, today the opportunities for learning how to be a competent mom are endless. So no matter what your background, you can acquire the skills you need to lead your children.

If you were going to build a house and had no carpentry experience, where would you start? You could become an apprentice and work with someone for a few months to learn about carpentry. You could read books, watch videos, and take classes. And you can do the same thing with motherhood.

Like most new moms, I made my share of mistakes, especially with my first child. The first time I took my son to the pediatrician's office for a checkup, he cried from the time we left home until we got to the doctor's office. It was winter and very cold outside. I wanted to make sure he was warm, so I swaddled him with enough blue blankets to wrap an entire nursery full of babies. When he wouldn't stop crying, I unbundled him and discovered why he was so upset: I had been holding him upside down!

Sometimes we make mistakes, but we learn to laugh about them, apologize when necessary, and move on. Other times we may not know how to help our children, so we have to ask for help. That help may come in the form of a mentor or family member; other times we might need to seek professional help.

STEP 3: Competence

Probably the best way to gain parenting skills and basic knowledge is to find a mom-mentor and learn from her. It doesn't have to be your mom, just someone who has successfully parented a child into adulthood. Think about it. Isn't there someone you know at church, at work, or in your neighborhood whose children exemplify the qualities you want your children to have? If so, use her as a resource for information.

If you can't think of anyone, there are dozens of places to meet possible mom-mentors. The homemakers' clubs I mentioned earlier include women of all ages, and they hold informative meetings about relevant topics in their homes. If your state doesn't have homemakers' clubs, ask your local chamber of commerce what groups are available locally for women. Keep in mind that many churches have women's Bible classes and often provide childcare for young children. If it's not possible for you to leave your home, why not invite several women to come to your house and study with you? Don't overwhelm yourself by thinking you have to clean your entire house and provide homemade snacks. If we only invite friends and neighbors over when the house is clean, we may have to wait for the kids to grow up and leave home!

Once you find a mom-mentor, don't be shy. Ask her how she survived colic and the terrible twos. Find out what she did when her children threw a temper tantrum in aisle five of the local grocery store. More than likely she will be glad to share! Just remember that ultimately you have to decide if what worked for her might work for you.

Sherrie is a good friend of mine, and her mom-mentor is a woman she met at church. Sherrie's mom lives on the other side of the country, and although her mother visits as often as she can, Sherrie found she needed someone close by whose advice she could access more easily. "At first I felt disloyal to my mother, like I was somehow betraying her by being friends with Jean," says Sherrie. "After I talked to my mother about it, she assured me she didn't mind sharing her grandchildren and me with Jean. In fact, they've actually met a couple of times, and they are friends now too."

There are also many agencies and clubs that provide information and support for mothers. For a comprehensive list of organizations as well as a recommended reading list, please see the list of additional resources in the back of this book.

Admit You're Not a Supermom

Women are by nature givers, nurturers, and caretakers, but there are times and circumstances beyond our control when we have to take off our cape and tights (I never liked those things anyway!) and admit we aren't Supermom. We don't know it all, and there's nothing wrong with asking for help. Sometimes we need more help than just a mom-mentor. Children with specific problems need specialized help. A major part of being a competent mother is knowing where and when to seek help.

When my elderly grandmother became ill, I took care of her. In many ways it was like having a child again. She was totally dependent on me and needed me to look out for her interests. The only difference between her and a child was that she was in her late eighties; therefore, her needs were very different. Still, I had to make all her decisions for her. Which doctor would she see? Should she get a second opinion? I had to watch her diet because she was sensitive to certain foods. I had to drive her wherever she needed to go. It was an awesome responsibility, and eventually it took its toll on my family and me. After a year of being in my care, my grandmother lost the ability to walk, and I could no longer lift her. When I tried, she would flail her arms and legs as if she were falling, and a couple of times, we both landed on the floor. I couldn't bear the thought of putting her in a nursing home, but I knew I couldn't go on the way we were. One of the last things I had promised my dying mother was that I would take care of my grandmother. To me, admitting I needed help was admitting defeat.

I poured out my heart to a friend, and she gently replied, "You will still be taking care of your grandmother, even if you have to have help. You are the one who will choose the facility that cares for her and the one who will visit her there. You are the one who will discuss her condition with the doctors and the nurses. You are the one who will bring whatever she needs in order to make sure she is comfortable. Neither your mother nor your grandmother would want you to neglect your family, and you can't do this on your own. You will still be in charge of her care; you just won't be doing it alone. You'll have a team of caring professionals to help you."

My friend was right, and her words were wise and comforting. My grandmother needed me to make decisions for her, just as young children need their mother to make choices for them. I couldn't do it alone, and there is no disgrace in asking for help.

Ask for Medical Help

There are many different reasons a competent mom may need help. Perhaps your child has medical problems or special needs. Even if there are no specific problems, selecting a pediatrician that's right for you and your child is extremely important, and it may require some time and effort on your part. Don't be afraid to conduct interviews and ask questions. Write down in advance any questions you want to ask the doctor so you will remember everything you wanted to know. Take notes so you can remember the doctor's answers and compare them to others you have interviewed.

Choosing a pediatrician is a big deal. In fact, your child's life could depend upon your ability to choose the right doctor.

When our daughter Rachel was seven months old, I took her to the health office for some routine vaccinations. That night she developed a fever. I called my pediatrician's office the next morning and made an appointment, even though I thought she was just having a reaction to the shots. The doctor examined her and told me to relax—it was the shots, and the fever would probably be gone by the next day.

A few hours after I got home, Rachel's fever was higher, and she became lethargic. Warning bells started going off in my head. (This brings up another important point: Trust your instincts! Go with your gut. If something doesn't feel right to you, do whatever it takes to get the doctor's attention. Remember, doctors are human beings just like the rest of us. They can make mistakes, so don't be afraid to be persistent if you feel something is wrong.) I called the pediatrician again, and something I said must have alarmed her; this time she told me to bring Rachel to the hospital immediately. When we got there, she took my hot, listless baby from my arms and felt the soft spot on top of her head. Then she whisked her away for a spinal tap. The diagnosis was spinal meningitis. I called my mother and father, and they were there within an hour. Our wonderful pediatrician spent the rest of the night at the hospital and checked on Rachel every hour. One week later Rachel came home from the hospital.

Was I glad I had chosen a pediatrician who was a good listener and who didn't mind if I called her when I felt like something was wrong? You bet I was!

Janice and Jim are the parents of Cheyenne, age six. Cheyenne was born with an extremely rare genetic disorder. Doctors were puzzled and gave Janice and Jim a long list of serious problems that Cheyenne would encounter. Several recommended institutionalizing her because, in their opinion, she would be severely mentally disabled. Janice and Jim were heartbroken, but they didn't give up on their daughter. They got on the Internet and researched other children with similar problems. Finally they found a doctor who specialized in genetic disorders like Cheyenne's, and he agreed to talk to them. He gave them a small ray of hope.

Even though they had never been on an airplane before, Janice and Jim bought tickets and flew from their home in Tennessee to Philadelphia. Now, almost six years later, they still visit the doctor in Philadelphia at least once or twice a year. Cheyenne doesn't look like most children, but she definitely acts like a healthy little girl. She communicates at and above her age level, and after several surgeries, she is able to walk. Cheyenne continues to get stronger and make progress far above and beyond her original prognosis.

Ask for Help at School

Michelle's son, David, didn't like school. In fact, by the time he was in fifth grade, he hated it. He had trouble concentrating, and it took him twice as long to complete his homework as it did his sister, Kendra. Michelle talked to David's teacher and guidance counselor. Neither was particularly concerned, and both told her it was probably just a stage he was going through. Doing homework with David meant a battle every night. Some nights it took him three to four hours to complete what his teacher said should only take about one hour. Michelle was stressed, David was stressed, and the whole family was suffering.

Michelle talked it over with her husband, and they agreed to seek professional help. They took David to a university in a nearby city, and David was tested for learning disabilities. The test showed that David clearly had problems processing information. The testing center did a complete report and offered suggestions for helping David. Michelle took the test results back to her son's school, confident that now they had the solution. To her surprise, neither David's teacher nor the guidance counselor was very impressed with the test findings. Michelle wasn't even sure they read the whole report, and the suggestions were never incorporated into a learning plan for David. The next year Michelle placed David in a different school, where the teachers and guidance counselor were more receptive. David did better and was happier than he'd ever been at school.

If your child has problems at school, ask for a meeting with your child's teacher. Again, write down your concerns beforehand, so you can refer to it during your discussion. You might forget something you intended to ask. Try to work with the teacher to come up with a plan that will directly address your child's problem. Offer your opinions, but be a good listener as well as an informed parent. If the problem doesn't resolve itself within a week or two, ask to meet with the teacher again. If you still aren't satisfied with the results, then go to the principal and guidance counselor and enlist their help. Then if that fails, look for resources in your community that might be able to help you. Colleges and universities are good sources of information. Ask friends and neighbors who have had similar problems how they handled things. Finally, don't give up!

Ask for Help with Discipline

"If you can't make my child behave at school, then how do you expect me to make him behave at home?" an angry mother yelled at an elementary-school principal. I happened to be at the school picking up one of my children when this angry mom let loose. I literally had to bite my tongue to keep from saying, "Lady, you've got it backward!" Discipline begins in the home.

I also know that even children who are disciplined at home can misbehave with the best of them. One of the worst shopping disasters I ever experienced happened when our twin boys were about three years old. I had taken them Christmas shopping, and we stayed in the store too long. They were tired and hungry, and when they reached for a toy and I said no, their emotions exploded. Both of them were on the floor, kicking and screaming and having what my mother would call a "hissy fit." I couldn't pick them both up at the same time. Two squirming three-year-olds are hard to hold on to. It only took a minute before I realized there was only one way out of the mess I was in. I unloaded all the items I had spent hours selecting and placed first one mad son and then the other in the shopping cart. It might have been December, but I was sweating like a politician on election day. I can still feel the glare the store manager gave me as I wheeled my screaming sons out of her store.

I learned several lessons from that experience. First, never take two three-year-olds shopping if you are going to be gone for more than an hour. Second, don't stare at women whose children are misbehaving; they feel bad enough without wondering if you are going to call Social Services on them.

Thankfully, that never happened again. Of course the twins didn't go shopping again with me until they were ten years old!

If your child has a persistent problem and you don't know how to handle it, don't panic. Somewhere there is a solution. You may have to be patient and diligently seek for an answer because some problems are bigger than others and some solutions are just harder to find. Remember Solomon's words: "What has been will be again, what has been done will be done again; there is nothing new under the sun" (Ecclesiastes 1:9). Whatever you are dealing with, you are not alone. Somewhere, someone has faced the same problem before.

Reach Out

There are many ways for mothers to reach out for help as we parent our children.

- *Seek help.* Sometimes other people have more influence over our children than we do, and that can be especially true when they reach the teen and preteen years. If your child has something on his or her mind and doesn't seem eager to talk to you about it, perhaps there is a mentor or a relative who can help. If so, don't hesitate to enlist help. Maybe someday you can return the favor. Do make sure it's someone you trust implicitly!

- *Stay calm.* When problems arise, we have a tendency to feel anxious, and that can actually make the problem worse.

- *Stay involved.* When I was a high-school teacher, I ran into lots of children whose parents had thrown in the towel. They felt like they no longer had control, so they threw up their hands and said, "My kid no longer listens to me. I can't do anything with him. He's on his own." It broke my heart, because without their parents to guide them, many of these lost souls got into serious trouble.

No matter what the problem is, no matter how old your children are, no matter if they don't seem to care what you think, stay involved. Search for answers. Try Plan A, B, and C, and then if you have to, go on to Plan D. There is always something you can do.

Eliminate the Fear Factor

Leaders who have God on their side have nothing to fear. To be competent, we can't be afraid of making mistakes. If we seek God's will when it comes to raising our children, He will lead us, and we don't have to be afraid. We can put our trust in Him.

Remember Deborah? She was a prophet who was one of the great leaders mentioned in the Old Testament. The story of her life shows how God can accomplish great things through people who are willing to be led by Him.

Deborah was the fourth and only female judge of Israel. When God told her to send for Barak and tell him to take ten thousand men to defeat their enemy—Sisera, commander of Jabin's army— that's what she did. But Barak let fear come between him and what God had told him to do. "If you go with me, I will go; but if you don't go with me, I won't go," he told Deborah (Judges 4:8). Deborah didn't hesitate. She went, but she warned Barak that because he didn't do exactly as God had instructed, the honor of capturing Sisera would be turned over to a woman.

Barak, Deborah, and their ten thousand men attacked Sisera's troops. The enemy's army all fell by the sword, except Sisera, who escaped on foot. He went to the tent of Jael, wife of Heber, and asked her to hide him and give him something to drink. She gave him a drink and a place in her tent, but when the exhausted Sisera fell asleep, she drove a tent peg through his temple.

It happened just as God had told Deborah it would. She had courage because she knew God was with her. We can have that same courage in parenting that Deborah had on the battlefield, if we are willing to listen to God's commandments the way Deborah did.

When the fear factor threatens you, read these verses for strength:

- "When I am afraid I will trust in you. In God, whose word I praise, in God I trust; I will not be afraid. What can mortal man do to me?" (Psalm 56:3–4)

- "Surely God is my salvation; I will trust and not be afraid." (Isaiah 12:2)

- "The LORD is my light and my salvation—whom shall I fear? The LORD is the stronghold of my life—of whom shall I be afraid?" (Psalm 27:1)

- "Do not let your hearts be troubled. Trust in God; trust also in me." (John 14:1)

- "So we say with confidence, 'The Lord is my helper; I will not be afraid. What can man do to me?'" (Hebrews 13:6)

- "Even though I walk through the valley of the shadow of death, I will fear no evil, for you are with me." (Psalm 23:4)

- "He will cover you with his feathers, and under his wings you will find refuge; his faithfulness will be your shield and rampart. You will not fear the terror of night, nor the arrow that flies by day." (Psalm 91:4–5)

- "So do not fear, for I am with you; do not be dismayed, for I am your God. I will strengthen you and help you; . . . I will uphold you with my righteous right hand." (Isaiah 41:10)

Worry and fear are two separate things. Was I worried when my daughter was ill and diagnosed with spinal meningitis? Of course I was. All moms worry about their children's health and safety. Worry should cause us to take action and seek help. By all means, do everything you need to do for your children, but entrust them to God, and relinquish your fears to Him.

Demand Respect

Part of my job at a local university entails working with students who are preparing to do their student teaching. Recently, Frank, one of my former students, e-mailed me to ask for my help. Frank is going to be an elementary teacher. He had signed up as a substitute teacher, but his first call wasn't for one of the elementary schools; it was for the high school. I could tell he was really nervous. "I've never worked with teenagers," he said. "Do you have any advice?"

I thought for a moment before I answered. "Always remember that there is a distinct difference between being a teacher and a student. Even though you are not much older than some of these kids, you are their teacher now. Act like a teacher. Be friendly, but don't act like their friend."

You can't act like an adolescent in a room full of teens and be respected. If a teacher doesn't have the respect of her students, she won't be able to teach effectively. The same thing applies to principals. They have to act like the principal, not like the students, or even the teachers. They are the leaders of their schools, and if they forget who they are, so will everyone else.

So it goes with motherhood. Your children don't need you to be their friend; they can and should have friends their own age. They need you to demand respect. They need you to be their mother.

My daughter went home with a girl from college once. When she returned from her weekend visit, I asked her if she had a good time. "Sort of," she replied. "It was really strange. Carol's mother wanted to be with us all the time. Where we went, she went. She tried so hard to be cool, and she even offered me a beer! It was totally weird."

Carol's mom was trying to relive her teenage years through her daughter. In order to feel young, she acted like a friend instead of a mother. As a result, she didn't gain the respect of my daughter, and she probably doesn't have the respect of her own.

Another way to lose our children's respect is by being afraid to stand up for what is right, even if it makes our children unhappy. For example, my friend Alice is a teacher who lives in another state. One day she called me and told me she was quitting her job. At first she was crying so hard I couldn't understand her. When she calmed down a little, I asked her to explain.

"We have a new principal, and he will do anything to keep the peace and make everybody happy. He can't stand having a teacher or a parent upset with him, so instead of making decisions that reflect our school policy, he 'fixes' problems himself," Alice said. "One of my students failed my class. I did everything in my power to help him, but he didn't want to be helped. He's a senior, and because he didn't pass my class, he wasn't going to graduate. His mother paid a visit to the new principal. Instead of supporting me, he told me to rewrite the test and make it easy enough that the student would be sure to pass it. He said our school didn't need Johnny for another year, and he sure didn't want to fight with the mother! I did as he said, but I won't work here again next year."

I didn't blame her. A leader who doesn't have the guts to do the right thing, even when it means making someone unhappy, isn't much of a leader. In the same way, a mom who gives in to her children because it's easier than doing the right thing isn't much of a mom.

My friend no longer respected her boss, so she couldn't work for him. If we want our children to respect us, then we have to do the right thing, even if it makes someone unhappy.

Don't Sweat the Small Stuff, but Pay Attention

My husband, Bill, is a wonderful man and great father, but his antennas don't function properly. What? You didn't know men had antennas? Sure they do, and you do, too, but there is a big difference between men's antennas and women's.

For example, Bill and I can sit down in the den to watch a program on television. Bill watches the program and quickly becomes engrossed in it. I watch and am distracted because my antennas are working overtime. The children are fighting behind the couch, and one is about to deliver a sucker punch to the other's stomach. I break up the fight and send them to their room. The dog is at the door scratching to be let out. I get the leash and take him out in the front yard. While we are outside, there is a low rumble of thunder. It's going to rain, so when I go back in, I close the windows. I hear yelling in the back and go to check on the boys. They are fighting again. I should have sent them to separate rooms. While I am in the room explaining the concept of "love your brother as you love yourself," the phone rings. It is a neighbor recruiting help for a church project. When I finally make it back to the couch and sit down by Bill, he grabs the remote, turns off the television, and says, "Wow, that was a great show, wasn't it?"

I don't think he even knew I was gone.

You see, his antennas point forward and stay fixed on the object in front of him, whether it's television or a task. If he's reading a book or working on the computer, he's focused—really focused. I, on the other hand, have rotating antennas that circle around my head and alert me to smells, sounds, and warning signals that Bill will never see or hear.

Moms have to use their antennas to detect danger when it comes to their children. They have to pick up the signals that something isn't right, because some problems that start out as small things have the capability of turning into big problems.

Take my friend Terri, for instance. Terri allowed her sons to have a computer in their bedroom with Internet hookup. "They're just nine and eleven," she said. "They don't even like girls, and they only use the computer for homework assignments.

I'm usually in the room helping them anyway. Besides, our house is small, and there is no other good place to put the computer," she reasoned.

Imagine her shock when one day she came home to find her two young boys visiting pornographic sites with an older friend who did "like" girls. When she checked the history list on the computer, it showed that this wasn't the first time the boys had surfed through dangerous waters.

"I never thought [the older friend] would do something like that. He goes to our church. I've known him since he was a toddler. He's been to our house numerous times, and the boys would go in their room and shut the door. I always thought they were playing cards or something. Then one day I realized the door was locked. I don't know why, but I didn't knock. I got the key and opened the door, and there the three of them were in front of the computer. I was devastated!"

Now the computer is in the kitchen, and the boys are only allowed on the Internet if Terri is sitting with them.

Bonnie's story is worse than Terri's. Her son Allan has a number of allergies. So when Allan started coming home from school with his eyes red and puffy, she chalked it up to spring allergies. A couple of times she thought she noticed a strange smell on his clothes, but he always had an explanation. Then his grades began to drop, and his personality began to change. By the time she and her husband realized what was going on, Allan was addicted to some very strong and dangerous drugs.

Use your antennas, all of them, when it comes to your children. If something doesn't feel right, smell right, or look right, trust your instincts. Remember the story I told you about my daughter's meningitis? Even though the pediatrician had seen Rachel that day and said it was a reaction to the shots she'd just had, something told me it was more than that.

Another time I had to trust my instincts, rather than listen to someone else's opinion, also involved my daughter Rachel. When she was in eighth grade, she went home with a girlfriend to spend the night. The next morning we picked her up on our way to our son's ball tournament in a nearby city. Rachel complained of a headache on the way to the game. I didn't have any medicine with me, but when we got to the game I asked my friend Betty for some Tylenol. I gave it to Rachel, and we settled in to watch the game.

After the game was over, Rachel was exceptionally quiet. By the time we got back to the hotel, she was acting very weird. Before long she began talking out of her head and not recognizing people she'd known for years. Bill and I left the other children with friends and rushed her to a children's hospital. By the time we arrived, she was nearly incoherent and vomiting. The doctors and nurses rushed her to the emergency room and began shining flashlights in her eyes and drawing blood. I tried to calm Rachel, but she was thrashing around so on the examination table that the doctors strapped her to the table. The young doctor examining her immediately assumed that Rachel had experimented with drugs.

"That's not what it is," I said, as I cried and tried to hold on to my daughter's hand.

"They all say that," he mumbled.

I knew my daughter, and I knew without a doubt that she hadn't willingly taken drugs. Someone could have given her something without her knowledge, I supposed, but I didn't think that was what was wrong either. I could tell by the way the doctor was talking to the nurses, he didn't believe me. I was furious and shaking so hard I could hardly stand.

"Fine," I said. "You don't have to believe me, but don't miss what is really wrong with her because you are so determined to believe my daughter is on drugs. Check out every possibility before you treat her for anything!"

I was so upset, I had the nurses go get my husband, who was taking care of the paperwork. I left Rachel in his care because they were going to do a spinal tap, and I knew I couldn't stand another minute in the room with the doctor who thought he knew everything. So while they worked on my daughter, I went to the bathroom and got down on my knees and prayed. Not the most sanitary place for prayer, but it was very private.

STEP 3: Competence

Many tests later Rachel was diagnosed with having experienced an acute migraine. We joked that there wasn't anything "cute" about a headache so severe it caused her to see colors, lose her ability to speak, and finally made her sick at her stomach. I was thankful to God that she was OK, and I resisted the urge to go find the doctor and say "I told you so," because I knew that, unfortunately, many of the children he saw in Rachel's condition did have drug problems.

Trusting our instincts means listening to that feeling deep down inside—the feeling that sets off warning bells in our heads. Some people call it women's intuition, but men can have it too. Mothers aren't only connected to their children by an umbilical cord. There's an invisible cord from a Mom-PhD heart to her child's heart that alerts her when something is wrong. With effort and care, it stays connected till death they do part. Sometimes it may become disconnected for a few years for one reason or another, but when reconnected the bond between mother and child is stronger than ever.

Don't sweat the small stuff, if it really is small stuff, but always remember that every big problem starts out as a small one. If your heart tells you there's a problem, don't push it aside just because someone advises you not to worry. They may have the very best intentions, but they aren't the mom. You have the final say-so when it comes to your child's well-being.

Find De-stressing Solutions

Positive Home Directors wear so many different hats that sometimes we need two or three hat racks to hold them all. The Virtuous Woman of Proverbs 31 was a homemaker, but she was a businesswoman as well. Whether we choose to work outside the home or stay at home isn't nearly as important as how we wear our various hats.

There has to be a balance between work and home. When one or the other gets to be too much, it's like trying to drive a car with a flat tire. It can be done, but it's a jarring experience! On the other hand, when work and home are balanced, things run smoothly; and when you hit a bump in the road, the tires help maintain a smooth ride.

A very good friend, we'll call her Debbie, started experiencing some disturbing physical symptoms. She went to a doctor who referred her to a specialist. The specialist informed Debbie that her condition was stress related. She was working more than fifty hours a week while caring for her husband and two young sons. The specialist advised her to cut back. At first, she didn't think she could. Her symptoms worsened, and her doctor then *ordered* her to cut back. Debbie told her boss about her problem, and they worked out a deal. He didn't want to lose a valued employee, and she didn't want to lose her job. Now she works fewer hours, travels less, and is a happier person. She did take a slight cut in pay, but she says the payback is more than worth it. All her physical symptoms disappeared within a matter of weeks!

For women who aren't as fortunate as Debbie when it comes to making compromises with their employers, there are other options—but be warned: you may not like them. Sometimes we have to make tough choices. We have to realign our priorities and make changes that affect the lives of the people we love the most: our families.

After my mother died, my father didn't relish living alone. My parents' house was huge, and our house was relatively small for a family of five, so Bill and I sold our house and moved in with Daddy. In addition to taking care of our three children, I was teaching full time, working on my master's degree, cooking for all of us, doing the shopping, paying the bills, and trying my hand at writing. Then the twins came along. Suddenly I had five children to care for, plus all my other jobs. When Daddy died in 1995 of a heart attack, it hit me very hard. I took a closer look at my life and reevaluated my priorities. Both of my parents had died at a relatively young age: Mom was fifty-one and Daddy was sixty-five. Did I really want to spend the rest of my life on a merry-go-round that was spinning so fast I wasn't sure I could get off?

I didn't, and Bill and I decided we could survive financially without my teaching salary. Still, it wasn't easy to quit. Coworkers told me I would be sorry. A friend cautioned me that if I stayed out of the job market too long, by the time I decided to go back to work, no one would consider me employable. In a way, letting go of my job was like taking a security blanket away from a child. I liked getting a regular paycheck. I liked teaching history. But I loved my family more, and I knew that my stress was affecting them. I saw a poster once in a store that said, "Before you can discover new oceans, you have to lose sight of the shore." I was terribly scared of losing sight of the shore.

I am not sharing this story with you because I think every stressed mom ought to quit her job. I was fortunate; by that point in our marriage, Bill was making enough money for us to live on. That wasn't always the case. I distinctly remember using some special silver dollars that a relative had given me to buy formula for my daughter. My pride wouldn't allow me to ask my parents for help, and I knew the coins were better spent feeding my daughter than sitting around collecting dust. We weren't starving by any means, but we had some lean years. I realize that most women don't have the luxury of being full-time stay-at-home moms. Looking back, I know now that those years were a learning experience for me. I was able to do things that before I had only dreamed about doing.

Because I was home more often, I could take care of my elderly grandmother and great-aunt. I could spend more time writing and searching for new markets for the pieces I wrote. And I could teach

Sunday school and work at Vacation Bible School without feeling like I was being pulled in a million different directions.

Once my children were older, I went back to teaching. First part time and then full time. At different ages and stages in our lives, events occur that can keep us from doing a good job of balancing work and home. It happened to me, and it may happen to you. Quitting a job isn't an option for everyone, but for those who do have a choice and who find themselves in a situation similar to mine, I want them to know there is no shame in leaving the job market, whether it's for a short time like me, or permanently, if you feel called to stay at home. The world will go on without you. *At work you are replaceable. At home you are not.*

Other options for balancing work and home include finding someone to help you. If your strength isn't housekeeping, a part-time maid might be the answer. Maid service may sound like an unaffordable luxury, but it doesn't have to be. Why not hire a teenager to help you clean for a couple of hours after work? They can use the extra income, and you can use the help. If you don't know any enterprising teens, ask around at church or in your neighborhood.

If you still can't find someone to help you, find a baby-sitter for a couple of hours and spend one hour cleaning and one hour relaxing. Take a nap, read a book, go for a walk. Don't get so busy that you don't spend time on yourself and your marriage. Plan a date night with your husband and stick with it. Not only will it strengthen your marriage, but it will give you some much-needed time together.

Take care of your physical, mental, and spiritual needs. You will do a better job of caring for your family if you take good care of yourself. Regular exercise and a nutritious diet are essential to lessening stress and living a healthy lifestyle. Whether you power walk at the park (my favorite) or join a local tennis league (my aunt's favorite and she's in her sixties!), exercise is a great stress reliever and a way to help maintain your physical and mental balance.

Suggestions for Single Moms

Single moms are especially challenged regarding time and finances. They need inexpensive ways to balance work and home. Here are some suggestions:

- Write out a budget and stick to it. Few things are as stressful as money problems. Having a budget and sticking to it will prevent falling behind on bills and payments.

- Seek creative day-care options. Churches sometimes help out with day care and provide baby-sitting services for single moms.

- Form a group with neighbors or other single moms and take turns baby-sitting each other's children.

- Carpool with neighbors. Not only is it cheaper for your children to share rides to ball practices and after-school activities, but it also gives you a break from being a chauffeur.

- Adopt a grandparent for your child. Many children live hundreds of miles away from their grandparents and don't have the benefit of getting to know them well. Find an older person in your neighborhood or church, and help your child develop a relationship with them. The right surrogate grandparent can make a wonderful role model for your child and help you out by spending time with them when you need some time alone. Just don't take advantage of them or expect them to be a free baby-sitting service. Nothing destroys relationships faster than the feeling of being used.

- Join your local YMCA. They have lots of activities for children during the summer and the school year as well. They also provide childcare while moms exercise. There is some cost involved, but it's reasonable and well worth it when you consider the health advantages of physical activity.

- Find appropriate after-school care. If you don't get home from work until hours after your child is out of school, finding after-school care is extremely important. Ask your child's school about programs they offer in the afternoons. Check with your local library, the YMCA, or the Girls and Boys Clubs of America. Somewhere out there is a program that's right for you and your child.

- Find something you and your child like to do and can do together. There are lots of things moms can do with their children that don't cost a dime but will strengthen the mother/child bond. Start a rock collection. Play a board game or card game. If your children are older, take them fishing or rock climbing. Find something you can do with your children that will keep the bonds strong during their teen years. You'll be glad you did.

SNAPSHOT OF A
COMPETENT WOMAN
Ruth

What would you do if there were a devastating famine in your country and your husband, father-in-law, and brother-in-law died? Imagine you are without any money and the person nearest and dearest to your heart, your mother-in-law, advised you to leave her and go back to your own people. Those are the circumstances Ruth found herself in. But when Naomi, her mother-in-law, asked her to leave, Ruth refused to go. Her answer to Naomi's request is one of the most beautiful and familiar passages in the Bible.

"Don't urge me to leave you or to turn back from you. Where you go I will go, and where you stay I will stay. Your people will be my people and your God my God. Where you die I will die, and there I will be buried. May the LORD deal with me, be it ever so severely, if anything but death separates you and me" (Ruth 1:16–17).

Life is full of problems. Ruth and Naomi certainly had their fair share. How we handle our problems defines our character.

Ruth lived through a famine, the death of several close family members, homelessness, and poverty. Yet she never left Naomi's side, and like Job, she never blamed God for her problems. Ruth's competency was founded in her trust in God.

Eventually Ruth married Boaz and gave birth to a son, Obed. Ruth is one of only four women mentioned in Matthew in the genealogy of Jesus.

With God's help and Naomi's guidance, Ruth survived tough times, and so can we.

Reflections on Competence

1. Can we be overly prepared for motherhood? Explain your thoughts and feelings. _____

   _____

   _____

   _____

   _____

   _____

   _____

2. Thomas Edison once said, "Many of life's failures are people who did not realize how close they were to success when they gave up." How can this statement apply to motherhood?

   _____

   _____

   _____

   _____

3. What happens when we try to be supermoms? _____

   _____

   _____

   _____

   _____

4. Many women (and men) have a hard time asking others for help. Why do you think that is and how can asking for help benefit us as mothers? _____

   _____

   _____

   _____

   _____

5. It has been said that women's intuition is a powerful and useful tool. Do you trust your motherly instincts or do you doubt yourself? Think of a time when you trusted your inner voice and you were right to do so. Share it with the group or your husband.

_____

_____

_____

_____

_____

_____

_____

_____

6. We all struggle with different parenting problems. What are some of your parenting hurdles and how well have you dealt with them. If you feel comfortable sharing with the group, discuss these problems and what you have learned from your experience. _____

_____

_____

_____

_____

_____

_____

_____

_____

7. Do you have a "fear factor"? If so, what frightens you about parenting? Is there something you can do to help you confront your fear and diminish it? _____

_____

_____

_____

_____

_____

STEP 3: Competence

_____

_____

_____

_____

8. How important do you personally feel it is for children to respect their parents and other adults? How do you teach them to be respectful?_____

_____

_____

_____

_____

_____

_____

_____

_____

_____

_____

_____

9. Are you an aware parent? What's the difference in being aware and nosey? Do moms have a right to be nosey, and if so, are there any limits? Is it wrong to spy on your children? _____

_____

_____

_____

_____

_____

_____

_____

_____

_____

_____

_____

*A word aptly spoken is like apples
of gold in settings of silver.*

—PROVERBS 25:11

Communication

leading with wisdom

*She speaks with wisdom, and faithful
instruction is on her tongue.*
—Proverbs 31:26

From the moment your children enter the world, you communicate with them. You talk and talk and talk, and then one day, they talk back! That's when the real fun begins. Years and years of sharing thoughts, emotions, and feelings are ahead of you.

Strong communication skills are a must for leaders, especially Positive Home Directors.

Listen to God

A conversation between two people involves talking and listening. Most of us do really well with the talking part, but we often fail when it comes to listening.

Remember Jesus's visit to Mary and Martha's home? Mary sat at the Lord's feet *listening*, while Martha devoted herself to all the preparations that had to be made. In their culture hospitality was a social requirement, and Martha was concentrating on fulfilling those obligations while Mary was enjoying her guest.

"She [Martha] came to him and asked, 'Lord, don't you care that my sister has left me to do the work by myself? Tell her to help me!'" (Luke 10:40).

That sounds like a sister telling on a sibling, doesn't it? There probably isn't a mother alive who doesn't have some "Martha" in her, but notice Jesus's response to Martha's plea for help.

"'Martha, Martha,' the Lord answered, 'you are worried and upset about many things, but only one thing is needed. Mary has chosen what is better, and it will not be taken away from her'" (vv. 41–42).

What a wonderful lesson for mothers! Do you consistently choose what is better, or do you stay "worried and upset about many things"? Do you spend the majority of your days and nights trying to clear clutter, do laundry, and scrub floors, instead of taking walks with your children or reading them bedtime stories or passages from the Bible?

Martha didn't do anything wrong. It was probably her nature as the older sister to be the one in charge, to see that things got done—and that's fine, as long as it doesn't interfere with what is really important: spending time with our Lord and our families. And remember what Mary was doing: listening to Jesus. How well do you listen to the Lord? Do you spend time communicating with Him daily? Do you listen when He speaks to your heart?

God listens when you speak to Him. The Bible tells us over and over that God hears our prayers and responds. "This is the confidence we have in approaching God: that if we ask anything according to his will, he hears us. And if we know that he hears us—whatever we ask—we know that we have what we asked of him" (1 John 5:14–15).

If God listens to us, shouldn't we listen to Him? He speaks to us through the Bible, and we listen by studying His Word. We can't know His will for us if we don't take the time to read, to pray, to reflect, and to *listen.*

Listen to Your Children

How well do you listen to your children? Listening involves more than our ears. When you are really listening to someone, you are still; your eyes are focused on them. They have your full and undivided attention. Too often we make the mistake of thinking we are listening when all we are really doing is hearing words. Solomon, in Proverbs 18:13, warns of the danger of not really listening: "He who answers before listening—that is his folly and his shame." A child's body language often reveals what their words don't say. If we are busy cleaning, talking on the phone, or driving the car, we may miss what it is our child is really trying to tell us.

One day I was busy cleaning and folding laundry. The phone kept ringing, and the list of things I had to do kept growing longer by the minute. Justin, our second son, was about five or six years old, and he was telling me a story about something that had happened between him and his older brother. The television was on, the dishwasher was roaring, and I asked him to repeat what he had just said. "I didn't hear you," I said. "Speak up."

He sat down in the middle of the floor, folded his arms, and stuck out his bottom lip. "I'm talking loud enough. You just aren't listening hard enough!"

We need to make sure we listen hard enough. It's the first step to being a good communicator.

Think before You Speak

Our words can be wonderful gifts that we give our children, like beautifully wrapped packages with big, fluffy ribbons. Or our words can be weapons that wound and scar the heart beyond the body's capability to heal.

"If anyone considers himself religious and yet does not keep a tight rein on his tongue, he deceives himself and his religion is worthless" (James 1:26). James goes even further with this idea:

"When we put bits into the mouths of horses to make them obey us, we can turn the whole animal. Or take ships as an example. Although they are so large and are driven by strong winds, they are steered by a very small rudder wherever the pilot wants to go. Likewise the tongue is a small part of the body, but it makes great boasts" (3:3–5).

When your tongue threatens to get the best of you, try visualizing it as a wild stallion and imagine yourself trying to ride it. Hold the reins tightly, and pull back with all your strength. We can't let our tongues go galloping out of control, or they will tromp right over our children's hearts.

I will never forget one busy morning when our twin boys were about four years old. I was trying to get to work, and I was running late. Grant was happy enough, but Russell literally wrapped himself around my leg, and he did the one thing that grates on my nerves like fingernails on a chalkboard—he whined. Have you ever tried walking with a whining four-year-old attached to your leg? It isn't easy. I quickly lost my patience and control over my tongue. I put my hands on my hips, glared down at my son, and said loudly, "Russell, I don't like it when you whine." He looked up at me and replied softly, "Mommy, I don't like it when you yell."

His words and the wounded look in his eyes were like a slap in the face. Which was more important: getting to work on time or giving my young son a few moments of my attention?

Thinking before you speak is just as important as your children get older. One of the most embarrassing scenes I ever witnessed took place in a high-school gymnasium. I was there to pick up one of my children from practice when a very angry mother came storming in to get her child. In front of the coach, the team, and other parents, she humiliated her child. "I told you to come straight home after school! You have work to do. We can't afford to run back to town and pick you up every day," the woman shouted. The young girl hung her head and followed her mother out of the gym. How my heart ached for that girl.

Thinking about what we say before we say it has other benefits as well. If we take the time to cool off and to speak calmly, we prevent those word arrows to the heart. Even when anger is not involved, being sure of what we want to say before we say it is still a good idea.

The other night my husband received an e-mail from a good friend. After twenty-five years of employment, a new manager had been brought in, and Bill's friend lost his job. Bill read the e-mail, told me about it, then got up and shut off the computer.

"Aren't you going to write Tom back?" I asked.

"Yes," Bill said, "but I want to think about what I'm going to say to him first. I'll think it over tonight and then respond tomorrow. I want to be sure I choose my words carefully."

Speaking without thinking can lead to reckless words: "Reckless

words pierce like a sword, but the tongue of the wise brings healing"
(Proverbs 12:18).

It's hard to imagine that adults would use their words like
swords to pierce a child's tender heart, but it happens. When I was
about ten years old, I was very chunky—not fat, but definitely not
skinny. One day I wore a lime green dress to school. It was a new
dress, and I thought I looked really cool in it. My teacher that year
was a woman who for some reason didn't like me. She took one
look at my dress and sniffed. "Well," she said, "one day you'll be
sorry you eat so much." I never wore that dress again. Even though
that was almost forty years ago, I still remember the sting of her
words.

We can't afford to be reckless with our words. We might just
pierce a heart that won't ever heal.

Choose Your Method of Communication Wisely

We live in a day and time where we have more choices of ways to
communicate than any other generation. Because of this, choosing our methods of communication carefully is more important than
ever. E-mail is great but may not be appropriate in every situation.
The immediacy of e-mail can also work against the "think before
you speak" rule. Remember Ecclesiastes 3:1: "There is a time for
everything, and a season for every activity under heaven." There is

also a way to communicate everything; and e-mail, because it is instant, is not always the best choice.

As a member of our local school board, I received an e-mail from an employee in a leadership position that really shocked me. After I studied it for a few minutes, I realized that it was written in a moment of anger. The author had vented her feelings and hit Send. Her message dripped with sarcasm and cutting words. Even worse, she didn't have the facts straight. The event she was referring to had not happened the way she interpreted it. She wasn't even at the meeting she was referring to! Even though I knew she probably regretted having spoken so hastily, my opinion of her as a leader had changed.

One of the most personal ways of communicating is sadly becoming a lost art. Is there anything more precious than a letter from a loved one in her own handwriting? My mother died more than fourteen years ago, and the most prized possession she left me was a box full of letters. While I was in college, she wrote to me several times a week. Those letters, full of her advice, wit, and wisdom, never fail to touch my heart. The very sight of her handwriting brings back so many memories. Handwritten letters touch us emotionally, and when we take the time to write a letter by hand, it gives us time to think about our words and choose them carefully.

During the teen years, it is critical to keep the communication lines open, but sometimes that's hard to do. I don't know how many times as a teacher I've had parents tell me that their kids "just won't listen to me!"

That isn't true. Our children may act like they aren't listening, but they are. They may ignore us and not respond, but if we are talking and they don't have headphones on, they hear us. They simply tune us out because we are saying something they don't like. Adults never do that, do they? Have you ever been to a business meeting where the speaker went on and on about things you either didn't have an interest in or didn't want to hear? I've been to a few faculty meetings where the people at the back table actually threw paper airplanes at their coworkers across the room!

Also, when you communicate with teens, remember that they don't like the words "no" or "I think you should . . ." That doesn't mean you shouldn't say them; it's merely a warning as to what might happen. If your teenagers are like mine, they will probably remind you of their age.

"What do you mean I can't go to the party? I'm sixteen years old!" Like I wasn't there when they were born.

When a teenager wants one thing and a mom wants another, sometimes the best way to communicate is through a letter. Write out how you feel and your reasons for not letting them do whatever it is they want to do. Try to stay away from trite phrases such as "If everybody jumped off a cliff . . ." Be original and creative. It will mean more. Then leave the letter on their pillow or where they will find it when you aren't around. Curiosity will force them to read it, and they can't argue with you if you aren't in the room. They'll read it and think about it. They still probably won't like it or agree with you, but you will have said what you wanted to say, and they will get the point.

By the way, this can work for kids too. Writing is a great way to vent anger. My daughter got mad at me once (actually many times) and wrote me a long letter about why I was a rotten mother. I kept that letter, and when she has a daughter, I plan to give it back to her. I'm betting that she'll understand why there were times when I had to be a rotten mother.

When I was a teenager (a few years ago), my mom would occasionally leave Erma Bombeck's newspaper column on my pillow. Mom loved to read, but she wasn't much of a writer, and so she let someone else tell me what she was thinking. I also remember several instances where I would come in at night and find my Bible open with a short note on a specific passage. I'm sure I didn't give her any indication that I read it, but I did, and I still remember Erma's words and the Bible on my pillow.

Remember Job? In a short span of time, he lost his livelihood and his children. Next he was afflicted with painful sores from the bottoms of his feet to the top of his head. What words of wisdom and comfort did his wife offer? "Curse God and die!" she said (Job 2:9). His friends didn't do much better with their words. They argued that Job must have sinned, and therefore he should repent. Not exactly the type of support Job needed, was it?

One thing that is noteworthy about Job's friends is that when they heard about Job's problems, they left their homes and went to comfort him. When they saw him from a distance, they could hardly recognize him, and they wept bitterly. Then they sat on the ground with him for seven days and nights without saying a word. That's right; they sat with him for a week *without talking.* They saw how great his suffering was, and according to Jewish tradition, people who come to comfort someone in mourning should not speak until the mourner speaks.

Anyone who has ever lost a loved one knows that not everyone has the ability to comfort those who mourn. After our father died unexpectedly of a heart attack, my brother and I greeted friends and neighbors at the funeral home as they came to bid our father a final good-bye. One lady walked up, took my hand, and asked me why the casket was closed. I was so shocked I don't think I even replied. Too bad she didn't know about the Jewish custom of remaining silent!

Sometimes silence can say more than all the words in the world. Knowing when to open your arms and shut your mouth isn't a last resort; in certain circumstances it may be the best way to communicate love and concern.

Often when our children are hurting we feel we must say

something to make them feel better, but perhaps what they need most is just our presence and a loving hug.

Set Clear Boundaries in Advance

Sometimes more isn't better, and when it comes to lecturing children, that's usually the case. There is a time and place for discussion, but if our children know what is negotiable and what isn't, then there will be fewer battles to fight.

We need to be sure something is worth fighting for before we make a big deal out of it. If we don't, it will be harder to be consistent with our actions—and *that* can cause serious parenting problems. Before we take action or communicate with our children, we need to stop and ask ourselves if this issue is something major or minor. If it's minor, let it slide. If it's a major battle, something that is truly nonnegotiable, go for it. If we aren't sure what to do, then we need to spend some time in thought and prayer *before* we communicate our feelings.

When our daughter wanted to get her navel pierced, I wasn't thrilled. She was seventeen and needed me to sign a form in order to have the procedure. At first I said, "No. Absolutely, positively not." Then the more I thought about it, the more I decided I was wrong. She was going to be eighteen in a month, and she wouldn't need my permission then. I asked myself why I didn't want her to get her navel pierced. Was it because I was afraid of what people would say? No, not really. Did I think it was a sin to pierce your navel? No. Then what was my hang-up? I couldn't come up with any reason other than I didn't like body piercings; and because I didn't like them, I didn't want her to have one. The more I thought about it, the more that didn't seem like much of a reason. If the establishment where she had the procedure done was clean and safe, why should I stop her? Especially considering that in a few weeks she wouldn't need my permission anyway.

So I moved navel piercing from the "major" battle category to the "minor." But I made a few things clear first. I told her that while I would let her pierce her navel, I didn't find it attractive myself and hoped she would think very seriously about piercing anything else. I also told her that tattoos were still in my major battle area and not to even go there if she didn't want me to have a nervous breakdown. I then told her that I had to approve of the facility where she got her navel pierced. If I did, I would sign the paper.

We went to the piercing/tattoo parlor (that's another story for a different book called *Never Say Never*), and I signed the paper. Imagine my daughter's surprise when I waved to her and told her I would wait for her in the car. "But, Mom," she protested, "aren't you going to go in the back with me?"

"I held your hand every time you got shots, IVs, or blood tests, but I will not hold your hand for something as silly as piercing your navel. You are on your own," I said and went to the car.

She paid for the procedure herself. She took care of the healing process herself, and she got no sympathy from me when her jeans rubbed against her new earring. A few months later, after her eighteenth birthday, she came home with her eyebrow pierced. She knew how I felt about the navel, but that was nothing compared to the way I felt about seeing my beautiful daughter's face with an earring attached to her eyebrow. I couldn't help it: I cried and cried and cried some more.

Then I got over it. Yes, I hated the earring, but I loved my daughter. If she wanted to be foolish enough to stick holes all over her body, I would have to come to terms with it. If she decided to get tattoos all over her body (which thankfully she hasn't), I would probably cry and cry some more, but eventually (hopefully) I would get over that too. It is, after all, her body.

Yes, we give birth to our children, change their diapers, kiss their boo-boos, and love them so much it hurts at times, but the bottom line is, once they pass childhood, they are on their own—or almost on their own.

My cousin Martha is a Positive Home Director who did a fantastic job of preparing her girls to stand on their own. Even when they were young, she let them make many of their own decisions. There were rules at her house, but when it was possible, she let her girls think for themselves. This gave them self-confidence and helped ready them for independence.

I was talking to another friend one day about how hard it was to let go of my teenagers. She said something that I have never forgotten. "One of the hardest things about parenting is watching your children trying to find themselves and seeing them fail. You want to run to them, pick them up, and fix everything for them, but that's the worst thing you can do for a teenager. They have to learn to pick themselves up, dust themselves off, and try again. They have to learn that every action has consequences."

She was right. It is hard to watch our babies (even when they are technically no longer babies) fail or do things we don't approve of, but we cannot always be their safety net. There comes a time when they have to walk the tightrope of life alone.

By the way, the earring in the eyebrow didn't last long. Not because of anything I did or said, but because of something that happened one day while my daughter was at the mall. A woman approached her about being a model for some event they were hosting in the city where she was attending college. "But you'd have to lose the earring. It takes away from your natural beauty," the woman told her. The earring disappeared the next day. I don't know who that woman was, but if she wants to call me and identify herself, I'd thank her and give her a big hug.

Be Consistently Consistent

If we have one set of rules for one child and a different set for another, we are sending a mixed message. All responsibilities need to be age appropriate, and each child needs to know in advance what is expected of him or her. Issues that concern age-appropriate activities, such as when a child goes to bed, may at first appear to be inconsistent to children; but obviously older children can do more and stay up later than a younger child. If you have a thirteen-year-old whose bedtime is 9:00 p.m. and a five-year-old whose bed-time is 7:00 p.m., the younger child needs to be told why the thirteen-year-old can stay up later.

The problem with consistency usually arises when we change our minds and thus change the rules. My friend Lora has a son who is often tardy for school. "I can't get him up in the mornings, and every day it's a battle," she said. "Finally I told him that if he was tardy one more time, when the weekend rolled around he would be grounded. Well, he was tardy again, and the weekend came. He didn't believe I'd stick to it. He begged. He pleaded. He whined. He made my weekend as miserable as he possibly could. Believe me, I wanted to let him go somewhere so I wouldn't have to listen to him! But I wouldn't back down because I knew if I did, he would be tardy again and again. We made it through that weekend, and so far he's made it to school on time every day since."

Be clear, concise, and consistent. Keep your advice short, sweet, and simple. Head off problems by having discussions and rules set up in advance. These are the keys to making your words like apples of gold in settings of silver!

SNAPSHOT OF THE POWER OF COMMUNICATION
Sarah

I can almost hear Sarah laughing now: "Sarah laughed to herself as she thought, 'After I am worn out and my master is old, will I now have this pleasure?'" Sarah was ninety years old when the angel of the Lord promised Abraham that she would bear him a son. Sarah thought that no one could hear her laughter—which communicated her lack of faith—but the angel heard and called her on it.

But her mouth betrayed her again when she lied about what she had done: "I did not laugh," she said.

Our words and the way we communicate, whether it be through laughter or a snide remark, greatly affect the people around us.

Even though Sarah was a woman of faith, she did not always have her tongue under control. She laughed at God's angel and then she lied to him. Her communications were a reflection of her heart. Instead of trusting in God, she considered the circumstances and said, "I can't." She forgot that even when we can't, God can.

There were probably many times when Sarah wished she had kept her mouth in check—especially after God's miraculous promise came true, and ninety-year-old Sarah gave birth to a son, whom she named Isaac.

Sarah wasn't perfect. She made her share of mistakes, but she loved her husband, and she was intensely loyal to her son, Isaac. She was the mother of the nation of Israel and an ancestor of Jesus Christ.

Sarah is also mentioned in Hebrews 11, along with other great faith heroes, as an example of powerful faith. "By faith Abraham, even though he was past age—and Sarah herself was barren—was enabled to become a father because he considered him faithful who had made the promise" (Hebrews 11:11).

This incident in Sarah's life is a reminder of how careful we need to be with what comes out of our mouths. Who we are is made clear by what we communicate. Let us prepare our hearts so that when our faith is tested, as Sarah's was by the news of her coming pregnancy, we will be in control of our words and reactions.

Reflections on Communication

1. Are you a good listener? Don't answer that question yourself. Work with your family or your husband or your other group members to come up with several qualities of good listeners. Then rank yourself (be honest) as to how well you meet these qualities. If you are really brave, ask others to rate you and don't be surprised if they don't rank you as highly as you ranked yourself! _____

_____
_____
_____
_____
_____
_____
_____
_____

2. Now list ways you can improve as a listener (to God, to your husband, to your children). _____

_____
_____
_____
_____
_____

3. Does your tongue ever gallop out of control? Name some dangers of an unrestrained tongue. _____

_____
_____
_____
_____
_____
_____

4. List the different methods you use to communicate (e-mail, letters, notes on the refrigerator, spoken words, etc.). Which method do you think is the most effective and why?_____

_____

_____

_____

_____

_____

_____

_____

5. What are some suggestions for getting teenagers to listen to us when they don't want to hear what we have to say?_____

_____

_____

_____

_____

_____

_____

_____

_____

6. Can you think of a time when the phrase "open your arms and shut your mouth" might be the best thing to do? Describe and discuss that time._____

_____

_____

_____

_____

_____

_____

_____

7. List some problems teens in your area face. Now think about your own children. Are these issues things you have discussed

with them frequently? Recently? How effective was your communication? What can you do differently next time? _____

_____

_____

_____

_____

_____

_____

8. What guidelines do you use to decide whether sometimes relating to your child is in the "major" or "minor" battle category?

_____

_____

_____

_____

_____

_____

_____

9. Was there someone in your life (not a relative) who was a good role model and influenced your life for the better? Describe their method of communicating with you about problems. What made you listen to them? Finally, consider being a mentor to a child at church or school whom you might be able to influence. Discuss ways mentors can change lives and then follow through by becoming one. _____

_____

_____

_____

_____

_____

_____

_____

_____

_____

You are the light of the world. A city on a hill cannot be hidden. Neither do people light a lamp and put it under a bowl. Instead they put it on its stand, and it gives light to everyone in the house. In the same way, let your light shine before men, that they may see your good deeds and praise your Father in heaven.

—Matthew 5:14–16

Charisma

leading with vigor

*She selects wool and flax and works with eager
hands. . . . She sets about her work vigorously; her
arms are strong for her tasks.*

—Proverbs 31:13, 17

What is charisma? I think of it as a special sparkle inside a person that drives them to do things with eagerness and vigor. When the person with charisma is a Christian, it's more than a sparkle—it's a light.

Some people, like my sister-in-law, Kelly, are born with an extra "charisma gene." She's an elementary-school principal, and when you walk into her school, the air snaps with electricity. If you are going to teach at her school, you had better be energetic and enthusiastic because she has high expectations for her teachers and expects them to have high expectations of their students. There are no cliques among the teachers, no "us versus them" mentality at her school. She genuinely loves her job, loves her students, and loves her teachers—and it shows.

There are many leaders past and present who are examples of the power of charisma. Could Billy Graham have drawn thousands to his sermons if he wasn't an exceptional preacher with charisma? And what about Martin Luther King Jr., John F. Kennedy, Franklin D. Roosevelt, or Winston Churchill? Certainly these men were great speakers, and their ability to speak in front of large crowds helped get them in the history books, but if they hadn't had anything important to say or if they hadn't delivered their message eagerly and effectively, would anyone remember what they said?

Having charisma doesn't guarantee you will be a great leader, but it almost always guarantees you will have followers. People admire charismatic leaders and *want* to be like them. Mom-PhDs with charisma have an easier time motivating and inspiring their children. Those of us who aren't born bursting at the seams with charisma, like Kelly, can take note of her characteristics and "copy and paste" them into our own lives.

Be Passionate

One of the main reasons leaders have charisma is because they are passionate about what they do. How effective would a teacher be if she didn't like children or teaching? How successful would a coach be who only coached because no one else would do it? How effective can a mom be if she isn't passionate about motherhood?

Stop a moment and think back to the years when you were in school. Who was your favorite teacher and why? I was blessed to have several great teachers, but my high-school English teacher, Mrs. Susan Chambers, stands out as one whose passion was inspiring. Mrs. Chambers made Shakespeare come alive in our classroom (even though I'm fairly sure he'd been dead for quite some time by 1970). She retired from teaching high school several years ago, but she's still teaching college English classes part time, and she and her family run a community theater in my hometown. Her children and grandchildren are all actively involved in the theater, and her present and former students continue to be inspired by her.

True passion is a lot like the Olympic flame—it just keeps burning and burning. It won't go out!

Passionate Positive Home Directors do their jobs with the same gusto and enthusiasm as winning coaches, inspiring principals, and talented English teachers. Being passionate isn't a guarantee that we won't get tired or discouraged or that we won't run into problems. It simply means that when hard times come, we keep on keeping on. We hold fast to God's unchanging hand and get through whatever lies ahead. And when things are good, we rejoice and thank God daily for the gift of motherhood and the blessing of having the most important job in the world!

Have High Expectations

Just as my sister-in-law, Kelly, has high expectations for teachers and students at her school, Mom-PhDs must have high expectations for their children.

Taking five young children to a restaurant that you don't drive through and get your food in a bag is a challenge. And when our children were young, we didn't dine out often; mainly because we couldn't afford it. But the few times we did all eat together at a restaurant, my children were well behaved, or as well behaved as young children can be. They didn't throw food, scream, yell, or get in major fights. One night after we had finished our meal, the waitress handed us our ticket and sighed with relief.

"Your kids were actually pretty good. You've got a lot of nerve taking all five of them out. I just have one, and I never take her anywhere," she said.

I thought about her statement on the way home that night. My children had been well behaved, and at least part of the reason was because I expected them to be. You've probably heard the expression "You get what you pay for." Well, with kids, more often than not, "you get what you expect."

Of course, there have been times when my children didn't behave as I wanted them to, but if children know in advance what behavior is expected of them, they usually (notice, I say *usually*) live up to those expectations. That rule doesn't apply if a child is exceptionally tired, hungry, or sick. Children have little or no reserves of politeness when they don't feel well. A wise mother never takes a tired toddler to the mall or a starving child to a restaurant where you have to wait for longer than three minutes to eat. Don't set yourself up for failure!

But if we expect our children to have good table manners, then we have to work on appropriate behavior at home *before* we go to a restaurant. We can't expect our children to behave well in public if they aren't taught how to behave in private.

Having high expectations for good moral character is even more important than having good manners. I have tried to teach my children to be kind and considerate. We take the golden rule seriously around my house, and we've repeated it to our children over and over again. At a volleyball game during my daughter's senior year in high school, I witnessed proof that she had been listening, although at first I didn't understand what was actually happening.

It was the last home game of the year, and while Rachel wasn't the best player on the team, she gave it her all. Because it was senior night, I expected that she would get more time on the floor than she usually did, but she didn't. In fact, she spent more time on the bench than she ever had before. I tried not to be disappointed, without much success. Rachel was a senior, and it was her last home game. Why hadn't the coach let her play? After the game I asked Rachel if she knew why she hadn't been put in. "Yes, I do," she said. "I told the coach to let Lindsey play. She hasn't gotten nearly as much time on the floor as I have this year, and her dad made a special trip from out of town to see her play. You've seen me play all year, and her dad hasn't been able to come to the other games. It just felt like the right thing to do."

I hid my tears until I got home, and then I got down on my knees and gave thanks to God for my daughter and the lesson of "do unto others" that she had just taught me.

Our children need us to have high expectations for them from the time they are born, because by the time they are teens, they have already formed many of the character traits that will stick with them throughout their lives. If we ignore a child's grades all through elementary school and middle school, then we inform him in high school that we expect him to go to college, we have waited too long.

Remember the family vision statement you wrote in chapter 1? Your expectations should be included and reviewed daily as a reminder of your ultimate goal.

We also have to start early and continually repeat to our children our expectations about drugs and alcohol. Even small, rural communities like mine are no longer isolated from rampant abuse of illegal substances. The other morning as I drove to school, I listened to a local radio station, and one news announcement after another mentioned methamphetamine. Just south of my hometown, a schoolteacher and mother of three was arrested for operating a meth lab in her home. And last weekend my cousins had to cut short their visit with my aunt when a sixteen-year-old friend of the family died suddenly. He had been at a party, and along with a few drinks, he'd taken a pill a friend gave him. He went home, told his parents good night, and never woke up.

Peer pressure is a powerful thing. One mistake can cost a child his life or create a lifetime of pain.

Voicing our expectations early and often is *not* a guarantee that our children will meet those expectations. But if we don't have high expectations and don't voice them frequently, then we shouldn't be surprised when our children fail to meet them.

Balance Charisma with Morals

If a leader has charisma but doesn't have good morals, tragic things occur. No one will ever forget Adolph Hitler. Certainly he had charisma. Thousands believed in him and were drawn to him because of his powerful speeches and his promise of hope for the German people. But he was responsible for the deaths of millions, and he destroyed the people and country he professed to love. Charisma without character is catastrophic.

Leaders must realize that because of their position they have a certain amount of power. That power can be used for good, or it can be used for evil. Many times leaders don't intend to abuse their position, but because of their own weaknesses or character flaws, it happens anyway.

Think about politicians who make the newspapers because of character flaws. The governor who resigned because he had an extramarital affair with a man. The congressman who had an affair with a young intern, who then mysteriously disappeared. These leaders never regain the status they once had.

Moms have to remember that when it comes to our children, we have a position of power. If we misuse this power, we may never regain our children's trust, and without their trust, it doesn't matter how much charisma we have, we won't be much of an influence in their lives. Not only do moms who abuse their position damage their relationship with their children, but worse than that, they endanger their souls.

"If anyone causes one of these little ones who believe in me to sin, it would be better for him to have a large millstone hung around his neck and to be drowned in the depths of the sea" (Matthew 18:6).

Charisma is desirable and attainable. If we love our children, we can work at being more enthusiastic. We can raise our expectations, and we can lead by example. But we have to remember that we are shouldering a huge responsibility, and only by following God's Word and His plan can we lead our children to Christ.

STEP 5: Charisma

Develop a Sense of Humor

That sparkle within a person that helps create charisma doesn't exist in people without a sense of humor. Life is serious business and parenting is a tough job, but it is also a whole lot of fun. Mark Twain once said, "My mother had a great deal of trouble with me, but I think she enjoyed it." I enjoy being a mom, and having a sense of humor does help when we have trouble with our kids.

Can you imagine life without laughter? It would be like living in a world without color, where everything came only in shades of black and white. Have you ever considered that if we want our children to be happy, we have to be happy first? The old saying is true: "If Mama ain't happy, ain't nobody happy!" It's true! Mom is the happiness thermostat of the home.

Children love to laugh, and nothing is more contagious than a child's laughter. A recent television commercial features thirty seconds of nothing but different children giggling. No matter how many times I see that commercial, it still makes me giggle too.

Laughter is not only the best medicine available, it is also a wonderful parenting tool. Why else would school principals make deals with students to kiss a pig if the students read a certain number of books, or something equally ridiculous? Because they know that all children love to laugh, even the big ones.

For several years I was a high-school history teacher. Talk about a challenge! History to teenagers is what happened last weekend—forget anything further back than that. Anyway, one of the things I learned from my teaching years was that teens absolutely love a teacher with a sense of humor. No, I didn't kiss any pigs, but the teachers did host an annual Christmas pageant, and several of us dressed up as ballerinas and performed a very embarrassing rendition of the *Nutcracker*. Keep in mind that we were all over thirty, some of us were tall and skinny, some short and not so skinny, but we all looked extremely funny in tutus!

Having fun and being playful is not the same thing as humor, but it's close, and it can work magic with children. My friend Julie loves going with her children to amusement parks. There is no ride too scary for her, and it's something she and her children can do together that they both enjoy.

Kelly, my sister-in-law, is the mother of three very active boys. When the oldest developed an interest in dirt bikes, she decided she'd like to ride with him. She bought a used dirt bike, and now the two of them trail ride together. She explains, "I realized that if I wanted to remain close to my boys, we needed to have common interests. Riding dirt bikes with my oldest son is a way we can spend time together and have fun at the same time."

No one is happy all the time, but a positive attitude, smiles, and laughter help make a Mom-PhD more approachable and a better leader. Don't feel guilty if you have a bad day now and then, as long as you're able to use your faith rope to pull yourself out of your temporary depression. Lots of great leaders had moments of self-doubt, and some were discouraged to the point that they wanted to give up.

Take a look at what these guys said when they were down-and-out:

- *Moses.* Poor Moses; he really had a tough time of it, didn't he? No matter what he did or God did, he just couldn't keep those Israelites happy. God gave them manna, and they wanted meat. In frustration Moses cried out to God and said, "Where can I get meat for all these people? They keep wailing to me, 'Give us meat to eat!' I cannot carry all these people by myself; the burden is too heavy for me. If this is how you are going to treat me, put me to death right now—if I have found favor in your eyes—and do not let me face my own ruin." (Numbers 11:13–15)

- *Elijah.* When hateful old Jezebel threatened to kill Elijah, the prophet ran for his life. "He came to a broom tree, sat down under it and prayed that he might die. 'I have had enough, LORD,' he said. 'Take my life; I am no better than my ancestors.'" (1 Kings 19:4)

- *Job.* If ever anyone had reason to feel down, it was Job. He lost everything that ever mattered to him in just a few short days—everything, that is, except his faith in God. But that doesn't mean he didn't get discouraged. "I loathe my very life; therefore I will give free rein to my complaint and speak out in the bitterness of my soul." (Job 10:1)

Each of these great leaders had moments of despair, but they bounced back. Moses eventually got the Israelites to the Promised Land. Elijah was rewarded for his faith by not having to face death, and Job was given back much more than was taken from him. These great leaders pulled out of their despair, and we can, too, by learning to rely on our faith and keeping a positive attitude.

Of course, there is a time for laughter and a time to keep silent. Teens don't like to be embarrassed in front of their peers. Cracking a joke at someone else's expense isn't humor; it's sarcasm. Young children don't understand it, and older children don't appreciate being made fun of. Leaders never use humor to make fun of someone; they use humor to inspire and motivate.

One of the most effective ministers I know is a man named Jimmy Bunch. Children and teens adore him, and one of the reasons is because he has a terrific sense of humor. He's not a comedian; he's a preacher—but he has learned that old and young love to laugh. He's funny, and yet he knows instinctively when it's OK to use humor and when he needs to be serious. He uses humor to lead people to Jesus, just like moms can use humor to lead their children.

Catch Them Being Good

Have you ever worked at a place where no one noticed when you did a good job? No one ever said thank you or recognized your efforts. Come to think of it, motherhood is sort of like that. But hang in there! Like the Virtuous Woman, your reward comes later, when your children are grown and rise and call you blessed.

Most businesses recognize valued employees in one way or another. They put a plaque on the wall for "Employee of the Month," or they give bonuses or raises. My husband's employer holds an annual banquet and recognizes employees who have been with the company for a certain number of years with small tokens of their appreciation.

What about our children? Do we recognize them for their accomplishments and achievements? Probably, if they win a tennis tournament or score high on a math test, we do. But do we notice when our son holds the door open for an elderly lady at a restaurant? Or when our daughter chooses to dress more modestly than her friends? Those are the character-building qualities we should notice but often don't.

When my children were just babies, my pediatrician gave me some wonderful advice that I've never forgotten. She told me to "catch them being good and praise them." That sounds easy, but over the years I noticed that it was actually easier to catch them being bad. Think about it: If your child brings home a grade card with four As and one F, which grade do you notice first? Which grade do you mention first?

When our children don't do as we hope or expect them to, they get our attention fast. Do they get our attention just as fast when they are good? If they don't, we are sending the wrong message.

Dress for Success

The Virtuous Woman was clothed in "fine linen and purple." What difference does it make what she was wearing? Have you ever seen a leader who dressed like a slob? We mentioned earlier that we didn't have a clue what the Virtuous Woman looked like, other than her clothes. While her physical appearance didn't matter, what she wore did. Purple was the color associated with royalty, and fine linen tells us it wasn't a cheap fabric. That doesn't mean all leaders wear expensive clothes. I doubt if Mother Teresa's wardrobe cost much, but she always looked clean and well kept. Considering the conditions she lived in, that probably wasn't easy.

Remember those commercials from the 1950s where women wore poodle skirts and high heels while they cleaned the house? Somehow I can't picture the Virtuous Woman in a poodle skirt or heels, or any clothes that weren't practical; but she took pride in her appearance and dressed well. Do we?

Jessie is a twenty-seven-year-old mom who experienced a reality check about her appearance.

After my second child was born, I found myself spending more and more time at home. It was just too difficult to take a baby and a toddler to the store. And when I did go out, I made sure my children were well dressed, but I just didn't care what I looked like. I didn't realize how much I had let things slide until one day I ran into one of Dan's business associates, Bob, at the local department store. "Jessie?" he asked. I could tell by the shocked look on his face and the way he said my name that he almost didn't recognize me.

I went home that day and took a long, hard look at myself in the mirror. I hadn't had my hair trimmed in months. I hadn't taken the time to put on makeup. Because I hadn't lost any of my weight from the last pregnancy, I was wearing an old pair of sweatpants and one of my husband's sweatshirts. Seeing myself through Bob's eyes was an awakening. I still need to lose a little weight, but I'm dressing better, wearing makeup again, and I never go to the store looking like I did that day I ran into Bob!

There is a time and place for everything, even yucky old sweats and T-shirts. No woman would dress up to clean house. The danger is in getting too comfortable in those clothes. We don't have to wear brand-label clothes or shop at expensive stores to look our best. But what we wear says how much we care. And if we care about being a leader, we need to look like one. Leaders are aware of the importance of their appearance.

Motivate and Inspire

Most little boys under the age of ten will tell you they want to grow up and marry their mothers. Little girls want to grow up and marry their dads. Why? Because they admire them. That blind adoration only lasts a few years, so we need to enjoy it while we can.

Although admiration is not the same thing as inspiration, one is essential to the other. You won't be inspired or motivated by someone you don't admire.

King David admired Abigail. He didn't care much for her husband, Nabal, but Abigail inspired and motivated David. First Samuel 25:17–40 describes how David and his men tried to be nice to Nabal, but he lived up to his name, since Nabal means "fool." Instead of saying to this armed group of men, "Thank you for your kindness," Nabal insulted them and their leader, David. Then Nabal went home, threw a party, and got drunk.

One of Nabal's servants went to Abigail and tattled on him.

"David sent messengers from the desert to give our master his greetings, but he hurled insults at them. Yet these men were very good to us. They did not mistreat us, and the whole time we were out in the fields near them nothing was missing. . . . Now think it over and see what you can do," the servant suggested to Abigail, "because disaster is hanging over our master and his whole household. He is such a wicked man that no one can talk to him" (vv. 14–17).

Abigail didn't waste any time. She got on her donkey and went straight to David, who had already decided to wipe out Nabal and all his men for his ingratitude. When she found David, she fell down at his feet and begged him to accept the gifts of bread, wine, sheep, grain, and cakes she had brought with her and to reconsider "needless bloodshed" (Proverbs 25:31).

David admired Abigail's courage. She motivated him to change his mind and not kill Nabal and his men. In fact, David was so impressed by Abigail that when Nabal died a short time later, David asked her to become his wife.

Abigail was courageous. What is courage anyway? One of my favorite definitions comes from Eddie Rickenbacker, who said, "Courage is doing what you're afraid to do. There can be no courage unless you're scared."[1]

We all face adversity. Abigail did, and we will too. We can look to God and find the courage to face our problems, or we can run and hide. Leaders use adversity to inspire others. Would FDR or Churchill have been as inspiring if they hadn't had to make tough decisions about World War II? One of my favorite movies of all time is *Sergeant York*. It depicts the true story of a country boy who, when called upon to fight for his country, couldn't decide if his religion would allow him to fight. He eventually went and became one of the greatest heroes of World War I. But you don't have to be a war hero or a president to inspire others.

When my cousin Martha was diagnosed with breast cancer, she was scared, and so were her husband and their three teenage daughters. One of her goals, besides surviving cancer, became to not let her illness take total control of her life. As much as possible, she wanted her daily life to proceed as it had before she was diagnosed with cancer. When radiation and chemotherapy treatments made her tired and ill, Martha still found the strength to go to work. Instead of walking around her fifth-grade classroom, she taught from the comfort of a recliner. She didn't try to hide her illness from her students. Instead, she enlisted their help, and there were many days when their love and concern gave her strength to carry on. Through it all she held fast to her faith and her family. When the cancer came back the second time, she persisted courageously, even though this time it meant having a mastectomy. Again, Martha's husband and daughters were with her every step of the way.

Because she included them in her experience, Martha's daughters learned some very important life lessons. They learned that it's easier to survive a crisis when you have the love and support of your family. And they came to realize that every single moment we share together is precious; there are no guarantees about tomorrow. They also saw Martha's unshakable faith in action. The way Martha handled her health problems was an inspiration to all who know her, especially her daughters.

Besides leaning on our faith and God's strength during times of adversity, we can inspire our children by our level of commitment to Christ, to our principles, and to the issues and causes we believe in. Besides being a wonderful Christian woman, my mother was a reading teacher and had a commitment to education that inspired not just me but also her students. Mom and Dad married when she was only sixteen, and I was born the following year. Three years later my brother came along. When my brother and I were both in grade school, Mom went back to college and got her degree. Because she had to struggle so hard to get her education, she encouraged my brother and me to get an education before we started a family. It never occurred to me not to go to college. Because of Mom, I knew I didn't have a choice. Not only did she make sure her children attended college, she strongly urged every child in her classroom to do the same.

Eight years after Mom's death, I received a letter from one of her former students. It was handwritten and three pages long. Jerry was one of those kids who didn't excel at sports and had a hard time fitting in. When he landed in Shirley Bell's sixth-grade reading class, he wasn't sure at first how he felt about reading or about his teacher, but it wasn't long until she had him reading about everything from King Tut to the *Titanic* and loving every minute of it. At the end of the year, when she hosted her famous annual party at her house for students who had read a certain number of books, Jerry won the trophy for reading the most books. "I still remember how many books I read and how I felt when I got that trophy," he said. My mother asked him what he intended to do when he finished school, and he told her he guessed he'd get a job. No one had ever told him he should go to college—no one except my mother. "You have to go to college," she insisted. "Look at your grades!" Over the years she encouraged him time and time again to go to college. He did and is now a registered nurse.

"I never told your mother how much she meant to me, even after I heard she was ill," he wrote. "Maybe by telling you, it will make up for the fact that I waited too long to tell her."

I still can't read Jerry's letter without crying.

When we truly believe in something and are committed to it wholeheartedly, we can inspire others.

SNAPSHOT OF
TWO CHARISMATIC WOMEN
Lois and Eunice

I have a deep appreciation for the enthusiasm and commitment of mothers of young children. As the mother of five, I know how difficult those early years are, especially on Sunday mornings. It takes a special kind of vigor and charisma to get small children up, fed, dressed, and to church. In my opinion, any mom who is capable of this is capable of launching a space shuttle.

When these courageous moms and dads bring their young children to church, we need to encourage them, especially those who launch the spaceship without any help: single parents. As hard as those early years were, I had my husband to help fetch, tote, and clean up. There are many moms who have no one. Those moms especially need our love and support. They need encouragement; yet many times they get the exact opposite. Most of the time it's not intentional, but a frown or disapproving look at a young mother who is struggling with a fussy child during a church service can be very discouraging.

Paul praises Lois and Eunice when he encourages his young charge, Timothy: "I have been reminded of your sincere faith, which first lived in your grandmother Lois and in your mother Eunice and, I am persuaded, now lives in you also" (2 Timothy 1:5).

While Eunice may have had the benefit of a mother who was a believer, the Bible says that Timothy's father was a Greek and is silent about his religion, which leads us to believe that he was not a Christian (most Greeks weren't). Paul says this to Timothy: "From infancy you have known the holy Scriptures, which are able to make you wise for salvation through faith in Christ Jesus" (2 Timothy 3:15).

Jewish boys in Timothy's day began formal study of the Old Testament when they were five years old, but not Timothy. Eunice and Lois began even sooner because they knew that God wanted them to train Timothy in His Word.

The next time a child cries or acts up during a church service, remember the charisma and commitment of Lois and Eunice. Think about how diligently they worked with Timothy. Praise all the moms and grandmothers at your church, and encourage them in any way you can.

Who knows, that little boy who cries during every Sunday service may be the next Timothy!

Reflections on Charisma

1. Do you know what you are passionate about? List your passions here and share them with others. What do your passions say about you?_____

   _____

   _____

   _____

   _____

   _____

2. List your expectations for your children. Are your standards within reason? Do they match the Bible's expectations for Christians? Do your expectations match your child's abilities and desires, or do your goals for your child reflect your own wants and wishes? _____

   _____

   _____

   _____

   _____

   _____

   _____

   _____

   _____

   _____

   _____

3. Name some leaders with charisma who attracted followers but didn't lead with integrity. What were the results?_____

   _____

   _____

   _____

   _____

   _____

   _____

4. How can a sense of humor help with parenting? Describe a time when humor helped you survive!_____

_____

_____

_____

_____

_____

5. Even leaders with charisma have moments of despair. Share a time when you felt despondent and then bounced back. What did you learn from that experience?_____

_____

_____

_____

_____

_____

_____

_____

6. How easy is it for you to "catch your children being good"? Describe the last time you praised your child for his or her character rather than for achievements at school or a sporting event.

_____

_____

_____

_____

_____

_____

7. If you had a friend who was like Jessie in this chapter and didn't care about her appearance, would you say something to her? Why or why not? _____

_____

_____
_____
_____
_____
_____
_____
_____

8. Who inspires you and why?_____

_____
_____
_____
_____
_____
_____
_____
_____
_____
_____

9. Look closely at the person you described in your answer to the last question. Do you have any of those qualities? Are they qualities you would like to have? If so, what is stopping you from being an awe-inspiring mom yourself? _____

_____
_____
_____
_____
_____
_____
_____
_____
_____
_____

*No eye has seen, no ear has heard,
no mind has conceived what God has
prepared for those who love him.*

—1 Corinthians 2:9

God-Centered Living
leading with faith

*Charm is deceptive, and beauty is fleeting; but a
woman who fears the LORD is to be praised. Give
her the reward she has earned, and let her works
bring her praise at the city gate.*
—Proverbs 31:30–31

My mother was only fifty years old when we learned she was dying
of colon cancer. That particular type of cancer is often curable if
caught early, but hers had advanced to her liver, and the doctors
told us she had one year to live. They were almost right: she died
the following July, fourteen months after we learned she was ill.
During her last days on earth, my sweet mother showed me that if
we are centered on God, we don't have to be afraid of anything—
not cancer or pain or needles or chemotherapy or even death.

My mother was also my best friend. Saying good-bye to her was
incredibly hard, but so was watching her physical deterioration.

When she died I was sad because I knew I was going to miss her, but I was happy she was no longer suffering. Because my mother lived a God-centered life, I also have the assurance of seeing her again one day in heaven. Losing a loved one, whether it is a mother, father, or child, is less painful if we have that hope.

My faith in God helped me accept my mother's death. It didn't keep me from mourning, but it reminded me that God has something better prepared for those who keep His commandments. Faith in God is also important to me because I realize what an awesome responsibility motherhood is. My husband and I brought five children into this world, and it's up to us to train them "in the way [they] should go" (Proverbs 22:6). There are no "do-overs" in parenthood.

That's why it's so important for moms to be God centered. We can depend on Him to show us the way. We can lean on Him when we are weak. And if we have faith in Him and do His will, then we will hear, "Well done, good and faithful servant" (Matthew 25:21, 23).

You see, if God isn't the center of our life, then something else will be. Whatever that something else is, it can't get us to heaven; and the alternative isn't something we would choose for ourselves, our children, or for anyone.

As women, the choices we make may affect a few people—our parents or, if we are married, our spouse. But after we become mothers, the choices we make affect our children as well.

STEP 6: God-Centered Living

Grow in Your Faith

To be God centered, we must have faith in God. Faith does not spring up overnight but is grown over our lifetime, but what kind of faith do Positive Home Directors need to grow?

First, we need to have a childlike faith. When people brought little children to Jesus to have Him touch them, the disciples rebuked them and tried to send the children away. Jesus stopped them. "He said to them, 'Let the little children come to me, and do not hinder them, for the kingdom of God belongs to such as these. I tell you the truth, anyone who will not receive the kingdom of God like a little child will never enter it.' And he took the children in his arms . . . and blessed them" (Mark 10:14–16).

To have a life that is pleasing to God, we don't have to have a college education or a lot of money. It doesn't matter what we look like or where we live. We simply have to be sincere and have a childlike faith.

We also need a faith that will sustain us, even in death. When I think of women with sustaining faith, I think first of my mother and the way she exhibited her faith during her terminal illness. Her ability to trust in the Lord every step of the way is something I will never forget. I find it amazing that she was able to show me her faith not only through her life but also by her death. She showed me the meaning of those familiar lines in the twenty-third psalm: "Even though I walk through the valley of the shadow of death, I will fear no evil, for you are with me" (v. 4).

Finally, we need to have a trusting faith. Another woman whose faith I admire is my friend Laura Kaye. She and I taught at the same high school, and once a week we would meet in her room before school for prayer. It wasn't long before I saw the tremendous inner strength that is directly connected to her faith.

Laura Kaye is the mother of three grown children: Whit, Tara, and Jody. While Tara was walking to her college class late one afternoon, a car struck her at a crosswalk. She was rushed to the hospital in serious condition. As soon as I heard about the accident, I called the hospital and asked for the intensive-care waiting room. Laura Kaye answered the phone. I was expecting her to be upset, and she was to a certain extent, but you would never have known it from the sound of her voice. Yes, she was sorry her daughter was injured, but she told me she trusted God and had faith in the ability of the doctors at the hospital. She asked for my prayers for Tara, informed me that she would see me soon, and hung up.

I was totally amazed at Laura Kaye's ability to remain cool, calm, and collected. Her calmness was a reflection of her faith, and I admire anyone who can remain calm under pressure. I don't react that way when trials and tribulations come my way, especially if they involve my children.

Act on Your Faith

Mark 5 records an example of the power of faith. A large crowd was following Jesus, including a woman who had been bleeding for twelve years. She had been to doctors and spent all she had, and still she was not well. In fact, she was worse. As she followed Jesus, she reasoned, "If I just touch his clothes, I will be healed" (v. 28). She reached out and touched Him, and her body was healed. Her faith had caused her to reach out to Jesus, even though she knew she was unclean and shouldn't touch Him. Jesus knew He had been touched, so He asked the crowd who had done this thing. The woman threw herself at Jesus's feet with fear and trembling and told Him the truth.

"Daughter, your faith has healed you. Go in peace and be freed from your suffering" (v. 34).

What if this woman had only thought about touching Jesus? Would she have been healed? Her faith caused her to take action, to reach out to Jesus.

Genuine faith involves action. If we say we have faith but fail to take our children to church, what good are our words? If we say we have faith but don't try to control our tongues, how can we be considered religious? Faith without action is like a car without wheels; it simply isn't going anywhere.

James asks the following thoughtful questions:

What good is it, my brothers, if a man claims to have faith but has no deeds? Can such faith save him? Suppose a brother or sister is without clothes and daily food. If one of you says to him, "Go, I wish you well; keep warm and well fed," but does nothing about his physical needs, what good is it? In the same way, faith by itself, if it is not accompanied by action, is dead. (2:14–17)

James continues by giving examples of biblical characters who put their faith into action. Abraham had faith, so much so that he intended to offer his son Isaac on the altar. Rahab, a prostitute, gave lodging to the Hebrew spies and sent their enemies off in a different direction.

Does it surprise you that Rahab is mentioned along with Abraham as a faith hero? It shouldn't. We might judge Rahab harshly and consider her unworthy because of her profession, but Jesus came to save the lost, all the lost, no matter who they were or what they did. He often shocked those around Him by talking to and visiting with those the world considered "undesirables."

Jesus doesn't care where we come from, what color we are, or what our profession is, but He does want each of us to believe with childlike faith and then do as James admonishes and act on that faith.

Tap into the Power of Prayer

Job is well known for his patience, but what about his parenting skills? We are told in Job 1:5 that he sacrificed a burnt offering for each of his children because he thought, "Perhaps my children have sinned and cursed God in their hearts." This was Job's regular custom. He wasn't sure his children had sinned, but he thought "perhaps" they had, so he went to God on their behalf. Notice, too, that the verse says this was Job's "regular custom," not just something he did occasionally when he thought about it.

I have to admit that having children greatly increased my prayer time. When they became teenagers, it increased again. One mother told me the carpet beside her bed was worn down because she'd knelt there so often in prayer on behalf of her teenage son.

I like to pray while I'm walking. Walking releases tension, and as the mom of five, sometimes I get just a little tense. I didn't realize my children had caught on to the fact that I "prayer walked" until one day after I'd gone walking for the third time. My oldest son looked at me when I came in and said, "Spending some extra time in prayer today, aren't you, Mom?" He was right; I was. I was glad he noticed, because one very good reason to pray is to let our children know where we go for strength.

There are numerous reasons to pray for our children. Job prayed for his children because they might have sinned. David prayed for his sick son to be made well. Prayer is our way of communicating with our heavenly Father. He wants us to come to Him!

Not only should we pray about our children, we should pray with them. Children hear prayers at church, but if they don't see and hear prayers in the home, they won't learn how to talk to God. Praying with our children also shows them that we value prayer and that we have a personal relationship with our Savior. And we never know how or when those prayers will be answered.

Patty was a widow who lived alone in Florida. Her only daughter, Angela, was grown and lived and worked in New York. Patty made friends with her next-door neighbor, Matt, who happened to be about her daughter's age. Patty was lonely, and Matt was a good listener and patient with the elderly lady. He frequently brought her groceries or ran errands for her. Patty would always invite Matt in, and invariably she would end up talking about her daughter. Patty showed him Angela's baby pictures and told him story after story about her childhood. She even introduced them to each other over the phone, and before long she began to plan for her daughter and Matt to meet. Angela would be coming home for Christmas, so Patty began to pray that God would bring the two of them together and, if it were His will, that romance would bloom.

A week before Christmas, Patty came down with the flu. Matt stopped by every day and called, but Patty declined to see him, saying she felt too bad for company. She assured him she had been to the doctor and was taking her medicine. A few days later, Matt received a phone call that changed his life forever. Angela had been trying to reach her mother all day, and there was no answer in her apartment. Matt took Angela's phone number and promised to call as soon as he spoke with Patty. When Patty didn't come to the door or answer the phone, Matt remembered he had a key and went back to his apartment to get it.

He hoped that he would find her asleep, but he didn't. Patty was dead. Evidently she was weak and had fainted, hitting her head on the edge of her dishwasher. Now he had to call Angela and tell her about her mother's death. Patty was more than a friend to Matt; he had come to love her like his own mother, and he struggled through his tears as he told Angela the news. Angela was devastated, and Matt did his best to comfort her. He helped her arrange a flight to Florida and told her he would be waiting for her at the airport.

Angela and Matt spent Christmas with Matt's family, and the day after that they held a memorial service. Together they scattered Patty's ashes in the ocean at her favorite seaside spot.

Patty's prayers were answered when, this past October, Matt took Angela back to that spot and proposed to her. Patty wasn't there to see her prayers answered, but somehow, Angela and Matt are sure she knows they are together.

So pray at mealtimes and give thanks for the food on your table. Pray at bedtime and ask the Lord to watch over your household at night. Pray in the morning and ask Him to guide your steps throughout your day. Pray with such faith that whether or not you see your prayers answered, you know in your heart that they were.

The more we pray, the closer we get to Jesus. By praying with our children, they will get closer to Him as well.

Trust and Obey

Earlier we mentioned fear as being afraid, but there is a second definition of fear. Fear of the Lord means to have a profound reverence and sense of awe toward God.

Proverbs 31:30 says that "a woman who fears the LORD is to be praised." The Virtuous Woman respected God, and because of that she wasn't afraid of anything else. She trusted God totally to lead her and to use her to lead her family to heaven.

"Trust in the LORD with all your heart and lean not on your own understanding; in all your ways acknowledge him, and he will make you paths straight" (Proverbs 3:5–6).

Notice that the verse tells us not to rely on our "own understanding." Any decision we make, any action we take, should be based on what He wants, not what we want.

Little children do their best to obey their mother because they love her. We are God's children through His Son, Jesus Christ. If we sincerely love Him, we will obey His commandments. To know what is expected of us, we need to read the Bible daily and study it closely.

Give God the Glory

Besides not leaning on our own understanding, Proverbs 3:6 tells us that we are to "acknowledge" God.

I know I couldn't have written this book without God's help, just as I know I am a better parent because of Him. Any honor for any accomplishments I might receive in my lifetime does not belong to me; it belongs to God.

Remember Deborah, the leader with charisma? She sang praises to God and gave Him the glory (Judges 5:1–31). Jesus's mother, Mary, also praised God. "My soul glorifies the Lord and my spirit rejoices in God my Savior, for he has been mindful of the humble state of his servant. From now on all generations will call me blessed" (Luke 1:46–48).

Be Fruitful

Jesus said, "No branch can bear fruit by itself; it must remain in the vine. Neither can you bear fruit unless you remain in me. I am the vine; you are the branches. If a man remains in me and I in him, he will bear much fruit; apart from me you can do nothing" (John 15:4–5).

If we have faith in Christ, we follow in His footsteps. We remain in Him.

What kind of fruit do we bear? "Love, joy, peace, patience, kindness, goodness, faithfulness, gentleness and self-control" (Galatians 5:22–23). Sounds wonderful, doesn't it?

Think of the fruit of the spirit as the benefit package for a Mom-PhD. Did the Virtuous Woman bear fruit and receive her benefits? You bet she did, and we will, too, if we remain God centered.

Cash In on God's Retirement Plan

Try to imagine what heaven is like. No pain, no sickness, no sadness, no laundry . . . Without a doubt, heaven is the ultimate retirement home.

Our mortal minds cannot envision the home Jesus has prepared for us. We don't have to; it is enough just to know He has prepared it and He's coming back for us: "Do not let your hearts be troubled. Trust in God; trust also in me. In my Father's house are many rooms; if it were not so, I would have told you. I am going there to prepare a place for you. And if I go and prepare a place for you, I will come back and take you to be with me that you also may be where I am. You know the way to the place where I am going" (John 14:1–4).

And the only way to get there is Jesus, who said, "I am the way and the truth and the life. No one comes to the Father except through me" (John 14:6).

Mom-PhDs have to be God centered to cash in on this retirement plan. Don't take my word for it; read about it in the Bible. Study about it at home and at church. Make God and His Son, Jesus Christ, the center of your life. *Forever* isn't a word that applies to anything in this life, but it does in the next. Jesus Christ is coming again, and you can be with Him forever; so can your children.

Be Prepared for Persecution

There is a very real danger that others will persecute you for choosing to be a God-centered mom. Jesus was persecuted, yet He still went ahead with His mission. He kept His eyes focused on His ultimate goal, and He didn't veer from His course. That's what we have to do too.

The devil is certain to shoot arrows at us. He may try to distract us with snide comments from people who are jealous or intimidated. He may tempt us with a high-paying job that would mean spending too many hours away from our children and husband. He has all kinds of ways of trying to divert us from Christianity, but if we take up our cross and follow Jesus, we can rest assured we will be leading our children to heaven.

SNAPSHOT OF A
GOD-CENTERED WOMAN
Hannah

More than anything Hannah wanted a son. Year after year she went to the temple and prayed. The Bible says she poured out her soul to the Lord, and the Lord heard her prayers and gave her a son. He also heard Hannah's promise: "If you will only look upon your servant's misery and remember me, and not forget your servant but give her a son, then I will give him to the LORD for all the days of his life" (1 Samuel 1:11).

For years her husband's other wife, who already had children, had mocked Hannah. When Hannah was finally blessed with a son, she was overwhelmed with joy. Yet her joy was mixed with anguish, since she had promised to give up the very child she had yearned and prayed for!

As the days turned into weeks and the weeks into months, the time neared for Hannah to wean her son—the time when Hannah had promised to return him to God. "They brought the boy to Eli, and she said to him, . . . 'I am the woman who stood here beside you praying to the LORD. I prayed for this child, and the LORD has granted me what I asked of him. So now I give him to the LORD. For his whole life he will be given over to the LORD'" (1 Samuel 1:25–28).

STEP 6: God-Centered Living

Hannah was a God-centered woman. Though it must have broken her heart to give up her son, she kept her heart centered on God, and she kept her promise. She prayed and gave thanks that God answered her prayers. Hannah loved her son and was thrilled to be a mother, but the focus of Hannah's life wasn't on her son; it was on God.

Reflections on God-Centered Living

1. Can you be a good mother without being God centered? Are there any dangers involved if moms are not centered on God? If so, what are they? _____

_____

_____

_____

_____

_____

_____

_____

_____

2. Does faith help us be better mothers? If so, how?

_____

_____

_____

_____

_____

_____

_____

_____

3. Describe how motherhood has changed your prayer life.

_____

_____

_____

_____

_____

_____

_____

STEP 6: God-Centered Living

4. List specific things you pray about in connection with your children. _____

_____

_____

_____

_____

_____

_____

_____

5. How do we know our prayers are always answered?

_____

_____

_____

_____

_____

_____

_____

6. How can we teach our children to give God the glory?

_____

_____

_____

_____

_____

_____

_____

7. Tell about a time you were persecuted for being a God-centered mom. _____

_____

_____

_____

8. Choose your personal favorite biblical mother and tell what it is you admire the most about her._____

_____

_____

_____

_____

_____

_____

_____

9. List the things your mother (or someone who raised you) did that reflect the leadership skills mentioned in this book._____

_____

_____

_____

_____

_____

_____

_____

10. Evaluate your leadership skills again and again. Underline the points in this book that speak specifically to your heart and re-read them. Use the Bible and this book to continually improve your Christian leadership skills. There's always room for improvement. If we are God centered, we can not only lead our children to heaven, we can lead others to Jesus._____

_____

_____

_____

_____

_____

_____

_____

Notes

STEP 1. Character: Leading with Integrity

1. Mother Teresa quote from her speech at the National Prayer Breakfast in Washington, DC, on February 3, 1994, found on http://www.priestforlife.org/brochures/mtspeech.html.

STEP 2. Compassion: Leading with Love

1. "Perseverance," *Life Application Study Bible* (Wheaton, Ill.: Tyndale, 1996).

STEP 5. Charisma: Leading with Vigor

1. Eddie Rickenbacker quote found on http://www.brainy quote.com/quotes/authors/e/eddie_rickenbacker.html.

Additional Resources

Books

Aldrich, Sandra P. *From One Single Mother to Another: Advice and Encouragement from Someone Who's Been There* (Ventura, Calif.: Regal, 1991). The subtitle says it all—advice and encouragement from a veteran single mother.

Aldrich, Sandra P. *Honey, Hang in There: Encouragement for Busy Moms* (Grand Rapids: Revell, 2003). A hundred and one short chapters to encourage mothers in their important role.

Barnhill, Julie Ann. *She's Gonna Blow! Real Help for Moms Dealing with Anger* (Eugene, Ore.: Harvest House, 2001). Helpful hints for dealing with the everyday pressures of parenting.

Bolton, Martha. *The "Official" Mom Book: The Who, What, When, Where, Why, and How of Motherhood* (West Monroe, La.: Howard Publishing, 2003). Humorous and poignant, uplifting and validating, this book reminds moms that they are important and irreplaceable.

Eller, T. Suzanne. *Real Issues, Real Teens: What Every Parent Needs to Know* (Colorado Springs: Life Journey, 2004). Advice from teens to parents.

Farrel, Pam. *The Treasure Inside Your Child* (Eugene, Ore.: Harvest House, 2001). Parenting tips for children of all ages. Also has helpful charts and activities. http://farrelcommunications.com

Jaynes, Sharon. *Being a Great Mom, Raising Great Kids* (Chicago: Moody, 2000). Jaynes shares key elements to great mothering. This book includes a Bible study for those who want to spend more time in study.

Ladd, Karol. *The Power of a Positive Mom* (West Monroe, La.: Howard Publishing, 2001). This book will lift your spirit and soothe your soul. Lots of suggestions for being a positive mom!

Miller, Kathy Collard and Darcy Miller. *Staying Friends with Your Kids* (Colorado Springs: Shaw, 1997). Advice for young moms on how to interact with their children.

Miller, Kathy Collard. *When Counting to Ten Isn't Enough* (Longwood, Fla.: Xulon Press, 2003). Biblical and practical encouragement for dealing with parental anger, including tips for disciplining children effectively.

Nichols, Fern, with Janet Kobobel Grant. *Every Child Needs a Praying Mom* (Grand Rapids: Zondervan, 2003). Encourages moms to pray for their children and gives them the tools to enrich their prayer lives.

Nixon, Brenda. *Parenting Power in the Early Years: Raising Your Children with Confidence—Birth to Age Five* (Enumclaw, Wash.: WinePress, 2001). Insights on raising a child from birth to age five, in three major sections: "Embrace the First Year," "Survive the Toddler Years," and "Maneuver the Preschool Years."

Shepherd, Linda Evans. *Teatime Stories for Mothers: Refreshment and Inspiration to Warm Your Heart* (Colorado Springs: Chariot Victor, 2001) An anthology of stories from moms who share their ups and downs, laughter and tears.

Bible Studies and Journals

Carmichael, Nancie and William. *Lord Bless My Child: A Keepsake Prayer Journal to Pray for the Character of God in My Child* (Wheaton, Ill.: Tyndale, 1995).

Miller, Kathy Collard. *Let Every Mother Rejoice* (Colorado Springs: Chariot Victor, 2002). This Bible study has ten lessons for individual or group study on topics ranging from releasing children to disciplining them.

Additional Resources

Organizations

Hearts at Home. Conferences for moms of all stages and many other great resources for mothers, founded by Jill Savage. http://hearts-at-home.org/new/.

Moms In Touch International (MITI), founded by Fern Nichols. Provides organizational tools to start a group of moms to pray for children in a specific school. The ministry's goal is to have a MITI group for every school in the world. Contact info: Moms In Touch International, PO Box 1120, Poway, CA 92074-1120; (858) 486-4065; E-mail: info@MomsInTouch.org.

Mothers of Preschoolers (MOPS). MOPS International exists to meet the needs of every mom—urban, suburban, and rural moms; stay-at-home and working moms; teen, single, and married moms—moms with different lifestyles who all share a similar desire to be the very best moms they can be! http://www.gospelcom.net/mops/.

Proverbs 31 Ministries. A storehouse of information for moms. http://www.proverbs31.org.

THE Mヲtherhood CLUB ™

Making a Difference One Kiss at a Time

mc

...born from a simple idea: *honor Mom for doing the most important job in the world.*

Titles included in **THE Mヲtherhood CLUB**:

Prayer Guide: *The Busy Mom's Guide to Prayer*
—Lisa Whelchel

Parenting: *Mom-PhD*
—Teresa Bell Kindred

There's a Perfect Little Angel in Every Child
—Gigi Schweikert

Inspiration: *The Miracle in a Mother's Hug*
—Helen Burns

Gift: *Holding the World by the Hand*
—Gigi Schweikert

Fiction: *Tight Squeeze*
—Debbie DiGiovanni

Devotional: *"I'm a Good Mother"*
—Gigi Schweikert

"At The Motherhood Club, you'll find books to meet all your mothering needs."
—Lisa Whelchel
(From *The Facts of Life*)